ALL

ABOUT

DEMOCRATS

 OVER 750 QUESTIONS AND ANSWERS

EDMUND LINDOP
AND
JOY CRANE THORNTON

ENSLOW PUBLISHERS, INC.

Bloy St. & Ramsey Ave.	P.O. Box 38
Box 777	Aldershot
Hillside, N.J. 07205	Hants GU12 6BP
U.S.A.	U.K.

Copyright © 1985 by Edmund Lindop
and Joy Crane Thornton

Library of Congress Cataloging in Publication Data

Lindop, Edmund
All about Democrats.

Bibliography: p.
Includes index.
1. United States—Politics and government—Miscellanea.
2. Democratic Party (U.S.)—History—Miscellanea. I. Thornton, Joy Crane. II. Title.
E183.L55   1985   324.2736   85-1530
ISBN 0-89490-104-4

Printed in the United States of America

10 9 8 7 6 5 4 3 2 1

CONTENTS

DEMOCRATIC PRESIDENTS
(including Democratic-Republicans)

1801-1809	Thomas Jefferson (D-R)
1809-1817	James Madison (D-R)
1817-1825	James Monroe (D-R)
1825-1829	John Quincy Adams (D-R)
1829-1837	Andrew Jackson
1837-1841	Martin Van Buren
1845-1849	James K. Polk
1853-1857	Franklin Pierce
1857-1861	James C. Buchanan
1865-1869	Andrew Johnson
1885-1889	Grover Cleveland
1893-1897	Grover Cleveland
1913-1921	Woodrow Wilson
1933-1945	Franklin D. Roosevelt
1945-1953	Harry S Truman
1961-1963	John F. Kennedy
1963-1969	Lyndon B. Johnson
1977-1981	Jimmy Carter

PROLOGUE:

THE BIRTH OF
THE DEMOCRATIC PARTY

When George Washington ran in the first presidential election in 1789, did he have any opposition?

No, Washington won a unanimous victory. There were 69 electors, and all of them voted for him.

How did the "Father of our Country" feel about political parties?

George Washington was strongly opposed to political parties. He was not alone. Most of the Founding Fathers, remembering the many quarrels during the Revolutionary War and recognizing that the new government they had formed was a radical experiment, feared that contesting political parties could destroy the young republic. When he stepped down from the presidency after two terms in office, Washington warned that party strife could lead to "riot and insurrection." He compared party rivalry to a fire that "demands a uniform vigilance to prevent its bursting into flame, lest, instead of warming, it should consume."

Nevertheless, political parties began forming while Washington was President. Why did this happen?

Two factions with different beliefs and goals emerged in the 1790s. One faction was headed by Alexander Hamilton and John Adams. President Washington, in spite of his opposition to factions, became aligned with this group. The other faction was led by Thomas Jefferson and James Madison. When these two groups publicized their ideas and began to bid for public support, they became our country's first two political parties.

What were the names of these early political parties?

The Hamilton-Adams group was called the Federalists. The Jefferson-Madison faction was called the Democratic-Republicans, or sometimes the Republicans. (These early Republicans were not related to the modern Republican Party, which began in 1854.) The name Democratic-Republicans was shortened to Democrats in the 1820s.

Did both these political parties advocate the democratic ideal of rule by the people?

No. The Federalists favored rule by the upper classes, the elite few who enjoyed the advantages of wealth and education. Federalist John Jay proposed that "those who own the country should govern it." The Democratic-Republicans, who had much greater faith in democracy, championed rule by the people.

However, when the Democratic-Republicans advocated rule by the people, they usually meant rule by white, landowning males. In the early years of our republic every state had qualifications for voting that generally restricted the suffrage to white men with a certain amount of property or income. When the Constitution was adopted in 1789, probably not more than 1 citizen in 15 could vote in the various states.

In the 1790s, which party supported a strong national government?

The Federalists wanted a strong central government and little power for the individual states. But the Democratic-Republicans, fearful that a dictatorship might emerge, believed that the best national government would be the one that governed least. They felt that most of the power should be held by the state and local governments.

Which groups in American society did each party favor?

Generally, the Federalists favored the prosperous business groups—the large merchants, bankers, manufacturers, and shippers. The Democratic-Republicans supported the farmers, town and city laborers, and small shopkeepers.

Some of the measures introduced by Alexander Hamilton, the first Secretary of the Treasury, were bitterly opposed by Democratic-Republicans as favoring the wealthy class. These measures included the creation of a United States Bank, protective tariffs and excise taxes, the Funding Act to redeem government bonds at face value, and the Assumption Act, which allowed the national government to assume the debts of the states. (Hamilton did persuade a reluctant Jefferson to line up votes in Congress for passing the Assumption Act in return for agreeing that the national capital would be located on the Potomac River. But afterward Jefferson claimed that the wily Hamilton had outwitted him.)

Did the two parties disagree about how the Constitution should be interpreted?

Yes. The Federalists believed that the Constitution should be interpreted loosely and that the national government had implied powers to establish policies and institutions, such as the United States Bank, which were not specifically mentioned in the Constitution. The Democratic-Republicans, on the other hand, said the Constitution should be interpreted strictly. One reason that Madison and Jefferson opposed the United States Bank was that the Constitution said nothing about the government creating such a bank.

When did the Democratic-Republicans run their first candidate in a national election?

In 1792, when George Washington was running for a second term. He was elected again by a unanimous vote, but the Democratic-Republicans tried to deny Federalist Vice-President John Adams another term. Against Adams they ran George Clinton, the governor of New York. Adams got 77 electoral votes; Clinton won 50 electoral votes. Already a sectional division between the two parties was developing. Adams carried all the northern and middle states except New York, Clinton's home state. But the Democratic-Republican candidate won all of the southern states except South Carolina.

When did the Democratic-Republicans first challenge the Federalists for the presidency?

In 1796. This election is discussed on pages 53-55.

How many Presidents have been Democrats (including Democratic-Republicans)?

Seventeen. (Although Vice-President Andrew Johnson succeeded Republican Abraham Lincoln as President, Johnson was a Democrat and is included among the Democratic Presidents. The names of these Democratic Presidents and the dates of their administrations are found on page *iv*.)

The modern Republican Party ran its first presidential candidate in 1856. How many Presidents have been Republicans?

Sixteen.

Who created the donkey as the symbol of the Democratic Party?

Thomas Nast, the political cartoonist, who also created the Republican elephant and the Tammany tiger. He drew these political symbols while working as a staff artist for *Harper's Weekly* in the 1870s. Nast himself was never a candidate for public office. He did, however, accept an appointment by President Theodore Roosevelt in 1902 as United States consul in Guayaquil, Equador. But Nast quickly fell victim to a tropical disease and died in Guayaquil on December 7, 1902.

PRESIDENTS:
THEIR PERSONAL LIVES

Grover Cleveland's first name was not Grover. What was it?
Stephen. Grover was his middle name.

Woodrow Wilson's first name was not Woodrow. What was it?
Thomas. His middle name was Woodrow.

Alexander Hamilton challenged what future President to a duel?
In 1797 Hamilton challenged James Monroe to a duel with pistols. He mistakenly thought Monroe had leaked some information to the press that forced Hamilton to admit publicly that he had had an affair with a married woman. A friend of Monroe persuaded the two men to settle their differences peacefully. Later, in 1804, Hamilton was killed in a duel with Aaron Burr.

What President's daughter, in a 1967 White House wedding, married a man who became a governor?
Lyndon B. Johnson's daughter Lynda Bird married Charles S. Robb, who became governor of Virginia in 1981.

What three Presidents died on the Fourth of July?
Thomas Jefferson and John Adams died within hours of each other on July 4, 1826, the fiftieth anniversary of the date when the Second Continental Congress approved the Declaration of Independence. James Monroe died on July 4, 1831.

Who was the youngest man elected to the presidency?

John F. Kennedy, who was 43 at the time of his inauguration. (Theodore Roosevelt was the youngest President; he was 42 when he assumed the position following the assassination of William McKinley.)

When he wanted to see something clearly, why did James Buchanan tilt his head to one side?

He was nearsighted in one eye and farsighted in the other eye.

What President's daughter married his Secretary of the Treasury?

Woodrow Wilson's daughter Eleanor married Secretary of the Treasury William Gibbs McAdoo in 1914.

Who was the first child born in the White House?

James Madison Randolph, the grandson of Thomas Jefferson, who was born on January 17, 1806. He was the eighth child born to Jefferson's daughter Martha.

Was Dolley Madison her husband's first love?

No. James Madison's first love was Kitty Floyd, who at 15 was engaged to the 31-year-old future President. Kitty lived with her father at the same Philadelphia boardinghouse where the bachelor Madison had a room. After a short romance Kitty called off this engagement to a man who was more than twice her age. Twelve years later Madison married Dolley, who was 17 years younger than her husband.

Who was the most recent President not to graduate from college?

Harry Truman.

What Chief Executive slipped away on a yacht so that he could have a cancer operation performed secretly?

Grover Cleveland. In 1893 a cancerous growth required the removal of his upper left jaw. The country was then in the throes of a financial crisis, and the President wanted to keep his operation secret so that it would not add to the public's anxiety. The operation was successful, and an artificial jaw was made for him of vulcanized rubber. However, Cleveland's speech was impaired, and he took lessons from a speech instructor before making any statements in public.

About two months after the operation, one of the doctors broke his oath of silence and leaked the whole story to the press. When the account appeared in a newspaper, the White House denied that the operation had ever been performed. It was not until 1917, nine years after Cleveland's death from coronary sclerosis, that another doctor revealed the full details of the operation that had been covered up for nearly a quarter of a century.

Who was the first President born an American citizen instead of a British subject?
Martin Van Buren, who was born in 1782.

Who was the first President born in the nineteenth century?
Franklin Pierce, who was born November 23, 1804.

Who was the first President born in the twentieth century?
John F. Kennedy, who was born May 29, 1917.

How many Democratic Presidents were born in large cities?
None.

What Democratic President was an indentured servant?
Andrew Johnson, who was indentured to a tailor. When Johnson ran away, his employer put an ad in a local paper offering a $10 reward for his return, but Johnson was not to be found.

Who was the lightest President?
James Madison, who weighed only about 100 pounds. He was also the shortest President; his height was 5 feet 4 inches.

Who was the heaviest Democratic President?
Grover Cleveland, who weighed about 260 pounds. But Cleveland was a lightweight compared to Republican William Howard Taft, who tipped the scales at between 300 and 340 pounds.

What President had a love affair with his wife's social secretary?
In 1914 Franklin D. Roosevelt fell deeply in love with beautiful Lucy Mercer, his wife's social secretary. When Mrs. Roosevelt discovered their love letters, she threatened her husband with a

divorce unless he agreed to end the romance. Roosevelt decided to give up his mistress, who later married a man named Winthrop Rutherfurd.

Who was with Franklin D. Roosevelt when he suddenly died from a cerebral hemorrhage at Warm Springs, Georgia, on April 12, 1945?

With Roosevelt at the time of his death were a woman artist who was painting his portrait and another woman, Lucy Mercer Rutherfurd, his mistress from many years before, who had been widowed. After FDR collapsed, Mrs. Rutherfurd left hurriedly, before Eleanor Roosevelt (who was in New York) and the press reached the scene. Many years later the public found out that the President had been with Mrs. Rutherfurd on the last day of his life.

Who was the only President who was never married?

James Buchanan.

What President was the first North American to grow a tomato?

Thomas Jefferson.

Who was arrested while he was President for accidentally running down an old woman?

Franklin Pierce, who ran down the woman with his horse. The arresting officer released the President after he discovered his identity.

What President was accused of living with a married woman?

Andrew Jackson. His wife Rachel was deserted by her first husband, who she presumed had divorced her. But two years after Rachel married Andrew, she learned her first husband had not divorced her. A short time later the divorce was granted, and then Rachel and Andrew were remarried.

Who was the first President whose mother could (and did) vote for him?

Franklin D. Roosevelt.

What President's maternal grandfather had been the mayor of Boston?

John F. Kennedy's grandfather, John "Honey Fitz" Fitz-gerald.

What President, according to legend, was confronted by a female reporter while swimming nude in the Potomac River?

John Quincy Adams. The story was told that a journalist, Anne Royall, was having trouble getting the President to give her an interview. So she studied his daily habits and learned that Adams went to the Potomac River every morning, stripped off his clothes, and took a brisk swim. Early one day she walked to the riverbank, sat down on the President's clothes, and refused to budge until Adams answered her questions. The persistent reporter finally got her interview.

What two future Presidents pitted their horses against each other in a race?

In 1788 George Washington entered his prize Arabian stallion Magnolia in a match race against a roan colt that belonged to Thomas Jefferson. Washington's horse lost, which may explain why soon afterward Magnolia was traded to "Light-Horse Harry" Lee, the father of Robert E. Lee.

Which President became an expert at both hunting and fishing and, after his retirement from public office, wrote articles on these outdoor sports for *Collier's*, the *Saturday Evening Post*, and the *Woman's Home Companion*?

Grover Cleveland.

Virginia is called the "mother of Presidents" because eight Chief Executives were born there. How many of them were Democrats?

Four—Thomas Jefferson, James Madison, James Monroe, and Woodrow Wilson. (The other four Presidents born in Virginia were George Washington, William Henry Harrison, John Tyler, and Zachary Taylor.)

How many of the seven Presidents born in Ohio were Democrats?

None.

The stone portrait of only one Democratic President is carved in Mount Rushmore, South Dakota. Who is he?

Thomas Jefferson.

To what young boy did Grover Cleveland say, "I wish for you that you may never be President of the United States"?
Franklin D. Roosevelt.

What is Jimmy Carter's favorite hobby?
Making wooden furniture.

What President invented a four-sided music stand, a dumbwaiter elevator, a revolving chair, a letter-copying device, and a cannonball-weighted clock that told the day of the week?
Thomas Jefferson.

What future President's fiancée probably committed suicide after breaking off their engagement?
James Buchanan's fiancée, Ann Caroline Coleman. The couple were engaged in the summer of 1819. That winter they broke off their engagement, and about a week later Ann died at her sister's home from an overdose of laudanum, an opium sedative. Buchanan wrote Ann's father asking to be a pallbearer at her funeral, but his letter was returned unopened.

What three Democratic Presidents graduated from Harvard?
John Quincy Adams, Franklin D. Roosevelt, and John F. Kennedy.

What future President courted the woman he married by playing musical duets with her?
Thomas Jefferson, who played the violin while Martha Skelton played the harpsichord.

What Chief Executive had been president of the same university that he had graduated from?
Woodrow Wilson. He graduated from Princeton University in 1879 and was its president from 1902 to 1910.

How were Theodore Roosevelt and Franklin D. Roosevelt related?
They were fifth cousins.

Whose wife died after he was elected President but before he was inaugurated?

Andrew Jackson's wife Rachel, who died on December 22, 1828.

What President was 18 years of age when he married?

Andrew Johnson. He fathered his first child at age 19.

When he was 23 years old, what future President wrote *Why England Slept*, a scholarly book about England's slowness to mobilize before World War II?

John F. Kennedy.

Was Franklin D. Roosevelt stricken with infantile paralysis while he was a child?

No. He was 39 years old when he was crippled by this disease.

What President had two brothers who died when their ship burned at sea?

Grover Cleveland's brothers, Richard and Lewis, died in 1872 when the S.S. *Missouri*, bound from New York to Cuba, was destroyed by a fire.

Who was the first President to ride on a train?

Andrew Jackson, in 1833.

What President and his brother piloted the sailboat that won the coveted McMillan Cup for their college?

John F. Kennedy and his brother Joe performed this feat for Harvard in 1938.

What President failed in the haberdashery business before turning to politics?

Harry Truman. He entered the haberdashery business with a partner in Kansas City in 1919, but two years later their business failed.

What three Chief Executives were born in the Carolinas but lived in Tennessee at the time they were elected President?

Andrew Jackson, who was born in Waxhaw, South Carolina, James K. Polk, who was born in Mecklenburg County, North Carolina, and Andrew Johnson, who was born in Raleigh, North Carolina.

What President never mentioned his wife in his autobiography, even though they were married 12 years and she bore him four sons?

Martin Van Buren.

What President's sister made her debut in London and married the Englishman who was slated to become the next Duke of Devonshire?

John F. Kennedy's sister Kathleen. Her young husband was killed in World War II, and she died in a plane crash when she was 28 years old.

What future President had a gall bladder operation without anesthesia at the age of 17?

James K. Polk.

What famous American author, after attending the inaugural ball honoring President James Madison, called the diminutive Chief Executive "a withered little Apple-John"?

Washington Irving.

What was unusual about a quarter-mile race between Andrew Jackson, the swiftest man in town, and Hugh Montgomery, the strongest man in town?

In this race, which took place when Jackson was a young man in Salisbury, North Carolina, Montgomery had a head start of half the distance but the handicap of having to carry a man on his back. Jackson caught his opponent near the finish and won the odd race by two yards.

Nathaniel Hawthorne and Henry Wadsworth Longfellow were the college friends of what President?

Franklin Pierce, who attended Bowdoin College and graduated in 1824.

Who was the first President to serve in the Navy?

John F. Kennedy. Ironically, the next four Presidents also served in the Navy—Lyndon B. Johnson, Richard Nixon, Gerald Ford, and Jimmy Carter.

Who was the first President to entertain the king and queen of Great Britain in the United States?

Franklin D. Roosevelt, when King George VI and Queen Elizabeth visited New York and Washington, D.C., in 1939. At an outdoor picnic President and Mrs. Roosevelt served the royal couple hot dogs.

What Democratic President was the most enthusiastic golfer?

Woodrow Wilson. Although he was never an expert at the game, Wilson frequently toured the golf courses in Washington, D.C. He played late in the afternoon or at five in the morning—whenever the mood struck him. In the winter when the fairways were covered with snow, Wilson played with balls that were painted red so they could be seen on the white ground.

The son of what President was killed in a railroad accident two months after his father's election?

Benjamin Pierce, the 11-year-old son of Franklin Pierce, was killed on January 6, 1853, when the train he was riding in toppled off an embankment. President-elect Pierce and his wife were on the same train, but they were only slightly injured.

What future President killed a man for besmirching the name of his wife?

Andrew Jackson shot and killed in a duel Charles Dickinson, a wealthy Nashville man, on May 30, 1806. Dickinson had made insulting remarks about Jackson's wife being an adultress.

Was Jackson injured in the duel?

Yes. Dickinson, who was considered one of the best marksmen in Tennessee, fired his pistol first, and the bullet hit Jackson. But Jackson was wearing a loose black cape, which deflected the bullet enough so that it struck a rib instead of piercing his heart. As Jackson started to drop to the ground, he fired, but the hammer stopped at half-cock. Jackson aimed again, squeezed the trigger, and this time killed Dickinson.

The future President felt no remorse about what he did. "I would have stood up long enough to kill him," Jackson later said, "if he had put a bullet in my brain." The bullet in

Jackson's chest was so near his heart that it was never removed, and he carried it the rest of his life.

What President once went ocean fishing for tuna and swordfish but landed a 100-pound turtle instead?
Franklin D. Roosevelt.

Did Harry Truman have a middle name?
No, but he had the letter "S" between his first and last names. Truman said that it should not be followed by a period because the "S" did not stand for a name. This unusual situation came about because both of Truman's grandfathers had names beginning with "S," so the letter was used to honor them both without hurting either one's feelings.

What was unusual about the epitaph Thomas Jefferson wrote for his own tombstone?
It said nothing about Jefferson serving as President! His epitaph read: "Here was buried Thomas Jefferson, author of the Declaration of American Independence, of the Statute of Virginia for religious freedom, and father of the University of Virginia."

What President as a teenager ran away to California, where he picked fruit, washed dishes, and did other odd jobs before he hitchhiked home?
Lyndon B. Johnson.

Who was the only President with an earned doctorate?
Woodrow Wilson, who earned a Ph.D. at Johns Hopkins University in 1886.

After the British burned the Library of Congress in 1814, what former President sold it about 6,000 of his own books?
Thomas Jefferson.

Who was the most recently born President?
Jimmy Carter, who was born October 1, 1924. John F. Kennedy was born in 1917, Lyndon B. Johnson in 1908, Richard Nixon and Gerald Ford in 1913, and Ronald Reagan in 1911.

Who was the first President to ride on a steamship?

James Monroe, who took a brief ride on the *Savannah* in May 1819. A short time later the *Savannah* became the first American steamship to cross the Atlantic Ocean.

What future President received a $1 million trust fund from his father on his 21st birthday?

John F. Kennedy.

What Chief Executive suffered a paralytic stroke while he was on a speaking tour?

Woodrow Wilson was addressing crowds across the country to stimulate public support for the ratification of the Treaty of Versailles when he collapsed on September 29, 1919, after making a speech at Boulder, Colorado. A few days later Wilson suffered a stroke that paralyzed the left side of his body.

What future President played on the freshman golf team at college?

John F. Kennedy, who consistently shot in the 70s at Harvard and usually in the 80s after he left college.

The pictures of which Democratic Presidents appear on the following coins: the nickel, the dime, and the half-dollar?

The nickel: Thomas Jefferson; the dime: Franklin D. Roosevelt; the half-dollar: John F. Kennedy.

The pictures of which Democratic Presidents appear on the following bills: $2, $20, $1,000, $5,000?

The $2 bill: Thomas Jefferson; the $20 bill: Andrew Jackson; the $1,000 bill: Grover Cleveland; the $5,000 bill: James Madison.

Two Democratic Presidents each had six children. Who were they?

Thomas Jefferson had five daughters and one son; Franklin D. Roosevelt had five sons and one daughter.

How many brothers and sisters did John F. Kennedy have?

Three brothers (Joseph, Jr., Robert, and Edward) and five sisters (Rosemary, Kathleen, Eunice, Patricia, and Jean).

Even though he had suffered a severe heart attack at age 47, what President worked every day in the White House from 6:30 A.M. until 1:00 or 2:00 the next morning?

Lyndon B. Johnson, whose only break in his grueling daily schedule was a short nap after lunch.

Who was the first President to graduate from the United States Naval Academy?

Jimmy Carter, in 1946.

What President battled a drinking problem most of his adult life and finally gave up his fight against alcoholism after his wife died?

Franklin Pierce.

What two Presidents had been widowers for more than 18 years at the time of their inaugurations?

Thomas Jefferson and Martin Van Buren.

What President ordered the construction of the first horseshoe court on the White House grounds?

Harry Truman, who frequently invited friends to join him in a game of trying to pitch ringers.

Who was the first President to cross the Atlantic Ocean while he was in office?

Woodrow Wilson, who sailed to Europe in December 1918 to attend the international conference that drew up the Treaty of Versailles.

With what President do you associate each of the following homes: (a) Monticello, (b) the Hermitage, (c) Hyde Park, (d) Hyannis Port, and (e) Montpelier?

(a) Thomas Jefferson, (b) Andrew Jackson, (c) Franklin D. Roosevelt, (d) John F. Kennedy, and (e) James Madison.

What President's mother joined the Peace Corps at the age of 67 and was sent as a nurse to India?

Jimmy Carter's mother, Lillian Carter.

What President bawled out a music critic for the *Washington Post?*

Harry Truman, who was furious when he read Paul Hume's

review harshly criticizing a concert performance given by the President's daughter Margaret. Truman wrote: "I have just read your lousy review buried in the back pages. You sound like a frustrated old man who never made a success, an eight-ulcer man on a four-ulcer job and all four ulcers working. I never met you, but if I do you'll need a new nose and a supporter below."

Why was John Quincy Adams attacked by his political enemies when he bought for the White House a billiards table, cues, and billiard balls?

They claimed it was an extravagant waste of public funds for items that were morally degrading. The cost was only $61, but the President's enemies created such an uproar that he finally paid for the sports equipment out of his own pocket.

After he graduated from college, what future President got a job teaching public speaking and debate at a high school?

Lyndon B. Johnson, who taught in 1930-1931 at Sam Houston High School in Houston.

The mother of what President, when visiting the White House, said she would rather spend the night on the floor than sleep in Abraham Lincoln's bed?

Martha Truman, the mother of Harry Truman. During the Civil War when she was a young girl in a Confederate family, Mrs. Truman had been briefly imprisoned at a federal internment camp, and she never forgave either President Lincoln or the United States government for the harrowing experience.

What President lived the shortest time after leaving the White House?

James K. Polk, who lived only three months after his presidency ended.

What President often entertained guests at the White House while wearing an old dressing gown and bedroom slippers?

Thomas Jefferson.

A contest was held for the architectural design of the White House. What future President entered the contest?

Thomas Jefferson, who wanted to be an anonymous contestant

and signed his plans with the initials "A.Z." The competition was won by James Hoban of Charleston, South Carolina.

What President had two sons who served in the House of Representatives from different states?

Franklin D. Roosevelt. His son James was a congressman from California (1955-1965), and his son Franklin D., Jr., was a congressman from New York (1949-1955).

When was the first attempt to assassinate a President?

On January 30, 1835. Richard Lawrence, an insane Englishman, fired two pistol shots at Andrew Jackson. Lawrence shot at the President from a distance of only six feet, but, miraculously, Jackson was not hit. Although the pistols had been properly loaded, for some unknown reason only the caps exploded. A gun expert estimated that the chance of both pistols misfiring was only about 1 in 125,000. Lawrence was taken into custody, was convicted, and spent the rest of his life in prisons and mental institutions.

What President-elect was nearly murdered while he was riding in an open car in Miami, Florida?

Franklin D. Roosevelt, who was riding in the car next to Chicago Mayor Anton Cermak on February 15, 1933. When the gunman, Giuseppe Zangara, fired at Roosevelt, a woman in the crowd grabbed his arm. The bullet narrowly missed FDR, but it hit Cermak, who later died from the wound. Zangara was captured and electrocuted March 20.

What President escaped death at the hands of two Puerto Rican nationalists?

Harry Truman, on November 1, 1950. At that time the Trumans were living in Blair House while the White House was being renovated. Truman was taking a nap when the assailants attacked. Hearing gunshots, he rushed in his underwear to an upstairs window to see what was happening. One of the Puerto Ricans and a guard were killed in the shootout. The other gunman was captured, convicted, and sentenced to death, but President Truman reduced the sentence to life imprisonment.

In 1979 President Jimmy Carter pardoned the would-be assassin after he had spent nearly 29 years in prison.

What former President was so poverty-stricken that on the day he died friends were seeking money for his relief?

Thomas Jefferson. On the day of his death friends were soliciting contributions for him at a ceremony in the House of Representatives celebrating the fiftieth anniversary of the Declaration of Independence.

What President's father served as ambassador to Great Britain from 1937 to 1941?

John F. Kennedy's father, Joseph P. Kennedy.

What was Harry Truman's boyhood ambition?

To become a concert pianist. As a boy, he practiced the piano two hours a day before going to school. After a recital he gave at the age of 14, a newspaper reviewer predicted that Truman would achieve musical fame. Many years later, after he became President, Truman gave a famous conductor his picture with this inscription: "From Harry Truman, who almost became a pianist."

When John F. Kennedy was a college student, did he plan to go into politics?

No. As a youth John F. Kennedy was quite shy and retiring. His family thought that the oldest son, Joseph, Jr.—who was outgoing and self-confident—would be the politician in the Kennedy clan. But when Joe was killed in World War II, John felt that, as the next oldest son, he should pursue the career that was planned for his brother.

What President wanted personally to arrest drivers he thought were speeding?

Woodrow Wilson. The President never let his own chauffeur drive his car faster than 20 miles an hour, and he felt that any driver who passed him on the road was a reckless speeder. Wilson was so vexed by this that he wrote his Attorney General asking if he had the power to arrest speeding drivers. Finally the Secret Service convinced Wilson that it would be neither prudent nor safe for the President of the United States to act as a traffic cop.

What President took a brisk two-mile walk every morning, twirling the gold-headed cane given to him by his Army buddies from World War I?

Harry Truman.

What President saved another man's life in the ocean by pulling him three miles to an island?

John F. Kennedy did this in World War II after his PT boat had been hit by a Japanese ship. Another sailor's legs had been badly burned in the explosion, so Kennedy put the man's life preserver straps between his teeth and dragged him to shore. The difficult swim took more than four hours.

What President had a magnificent collection of stamps and also collected naval prints and ship models?

Franklin D. Roosevelt. After his death, his personal stamp collection was sold for more than $200,000.

Why did John F. Kennedy appear at his wedding with large scratches covering his face?

Because the day before, when playing touch football with his family, he had fallen into a rosebush while trying to catch a pass.

What President was accused of fathering several children by Sally Hemings, a beautiful black slave?

Thomas Jefferson. Hemings was a slave who lived on Jefferson's plantation, but historians disagree as to whether Jefferson kept her as a mistress and whether he fathered any of her five children.

What two Presidents both tried out for the position of end on the freshman football team at the same university?

Franklin D. Roosevelt and John F. Kennedy both tried out for end on the freshman team at Harvard. Roosevelt, weighing only 146 pounds, lasted only two weeks, but he did manage to become captain of one of the scrub teams that played against the varsity in practice games. Through dogged persistence

Kennedy made the squad, but he was dropped to the junior varsity in his sophomore year.

What future President was nearly murdered as he returned home from Abraham Lincoln's inauguration in 1861?

Andrew Johnson of Tennessee, who was the only Southern senator to oppose secession. When he was homeward bound after Lincoln's inauguration, an angry mob of secessionists boarded his train at Liberty, Virginia, and Johnson had to brandish his revolver to force them off the train. He was in even greater danger when the train stopped at Lynchburg, Virginia. There another mob dragged Johnson from the train, kicked him, spat on him, and was ready to hang him when someone in the crowd called out that the people of Tennessee should be given the pleasure of putting their "traitor" to death. After Johnson returned to his home state, he was threatened many times, but he courageously spoke out at public meetings for the Union cause, sometimes with his revolver resting on the rostrum. In June 1861 Tennessee voted to join the Confederacy, and Johnson fled the state before he could be captured.

What President's father had been a linen weaver in Ireland?

Andrew Jackson's father, who was also named Andrew Jackson.

Who was the only President to win a Pulitzer Prize?

John F. Kennedy was awarded the 1957 Pulitzer Prize for biography for *Profiles in Courage*. Some of his scholarly associates helped Kennedy research and write the book.

When he was a student at college, what President sang tenor in the glee club?

Woodrow Wilson. He had a pleasing voice, and when the Princeton Glee Club performed, he usually sang several solos. Later, when he was governor of New Jersey, Wilson entertained politicians at a dinner by singing beautifully several black spirituals.

"Listen to the Mockingbird," a very popular song in the 1800s, was dedicated to what President's niece?

It was dedicated to James Buchanan's niece, Harriet Lane, who was the White House hostess for her bachelor uncle. Young, attractive, and energetic, Harriet Lane enjoyed entertaining. In 1860 she escorted the visiting Prince of Wales to a school for girls, where he played tenpins.

At a White House dinner honoring Nobel Prize winners, what President said, "I believe this is the most extraordinary collection of talent, of human knowledge, that has ever been gathered together at the White House, with the possible exception of when Thomas Jefferson dined alone"?

John F. Kennedy.

What three Democratic Presidents lived into their eighties?

Harry Truman: 88 years, James Madison: 85 years, and Thomas Jefferson: 83 years.

What future President helped coach football at two universities?

While he was a professor of history and political science, Woodrow Wilson helped coach the football teams at Wesleyan and Princeton. This was during the 1880s and 1890s, before universities hired regular full-time football coaches.

What President called another President "the White House's most distinguished pianist"?

Richard Nixon said this to Harry Truman in 1969 when he presented the former President's White House piano to the Truman Library in Independence, Missouri. Then Nixon sat down at the piano and in Truman's honor played "The Missouri Waltz." Little did Nixon realize that Truman detested this song. But the ex-President was then 84 years of age and so hard of hearing that after Nixon's rendition he turned to Mrs. Truman and asked, "What piece was that?"

What President wrote a movie script based on the story of the famous ship the *Constitution* ("Old Ironsides")?

Franklin D. Roosevelt, but he never succeeded in selling his script to a Hollywood studio.

What President invited all of the nation's leading composers and conductors to a White House concert featuring Pablo Casals, the world-renowned cellist?

John F. Kennedy, in November 1961.

What future President was the first member of Congress to enlist in the armed forces in World War II?

Congressman Lyndon B. Johnson, who was commissioned as a lieutenant commander in the Navy two days after Pearl Harbor.

How did John F. Kennedy get the severe spinal injury that led to two serious operations and caused him great pain during most of his adult life?

Kennedy received the injury while playing football as a sophomore at Harvard. It was aggravated in World War II when his PT boat was rammed and cut in half by a Japanese destroyer. His two spinal operations were in 1954 and 1955 while he was serving in the United States Senate.

Who was the only President to become a published poet?

John Quincy Adams, who in 1832 published a 108-page book of his poetry. His eldest son, George Washington Adams, wanted to be a professional poet, but he suffered from severe psychological problems and was lost at sea (a possible suicide) at age 28.

What President kept a string of racehorses that were entered in many match races?

Andrew Jackson, who personally trained his own thoroughbreds when he had the time. His most famous horse, Truxton, won at least $20,000 in races.

Which President enjoyed swimming nude in the White House pool?

Lyndon B. Johnson.

What are Jimmy Carter's favorite sports?

Jogging, fishing, tennis, and softball.

Why did Franklin D. Roosevelt spend as much time as he could at Warm Springs, Georgia?

Roosevelt exercised strenuously to overcome the crippling effects of infantile paralysis, but he never regained much use of his legs. So he was enthusiastic when, during his convalescence, he discovered the mineral springs pool at Warm Springs. Swimming in the pool, he claimed, made him feel stronger. Other handicapped people heard of his endorsement and began flocking to Warm Springs. In 1926 FDR bought the spa and incorporated it as a nonprofit foundation. He visited there so frequently that his cottage at Warm Springs became known as "the Little White House."

At his first state dinner what President had a musical program that combined Italian opera with a hootenanny from the American West?

Lyndon B. Johnson. At this dinner honoring the President of Italy, Robert Merrill from the Metropolitan Opera sang arias from *La Traviata* and *The Barber of Seville*, followed by the New Christy Minstrels strumming guitars and warbling folk songs.

How many Democratic Presidents are buried at Arlington National Cemetery?

Only one, John F. Kennedy. (Republican William Howard Taft is also buried there.)

PRESIDENTS:

THEIR PUBLIC CAREERS

How many of the first six Democratic Presidents had been Secretary of State in previous administrations?

All of them except Andrew Jackson. Thomas Jefferson had been Secretary of State in George Washington's administration, James Madison in Jefferson's administration, James Monroe in Madison's administration, John Quincy Adams in Monroe's administration, and Martin Van Buren in Jackson's administration.

How many Republican Presidents had been Secretary of State?

None.

Who was the last Secretary of State to become President?

James Buchanan, who was Secretary of State in James K. Polk's administration, from 1845 to 1849.

What four Democratic Vice-Presidents later were elected to the presidency?

Thomas Jefferson in 1800 and 1804, Martin Van Buren in 1836, Harry Truman in 1948, and Lyndon B. Johnson in 1964.

What prominent role did Thomas Jefferson play at the Second Continental Congress?

He was chief author of the Declaration of Independence.

Did Jefferson also play a major role at the Constitutional Convention?

No. During the time that the Constitutional Convention met, Jefferson was minister to France from the Articles of Confederation government.

What two future Presidents signed the Constitution?

George Washington and James Madison.

Who was the first senator elected to the presidency?

James Monroe, who served as a senator from Virginia from 1790 to 1794.

Who was the first member of the House of Representatives elected to the presidency?

James Madison, who was elected from Virginia to the first session of the House of Representatives in 1789. He served in the House until 1797, where he helped write the Bill of Rights and led the attack on some of Secretary of the Treasury Alexander Hamilton's economic measures, including the First United States Bank.

Who was the first governor to be elected President?

Thomas Jefferson, who was governor of Virginia from 1779 to 1781, during the Revolutionary War. He moved the capital of Virginia from Williamsburg to Richmond, but he was unable to protect his state from British invasion.

Who was the only former President ever elected to the Senate?

Andrew Johnson. He left the White House in 1869, and five years later he campaigned in Tennessee for senator and won. In 1875 he took his seat in the Senate, which he had left 13 years before. Johnson thus became the only ex-President ever elected to the Senate. However, he served only a few months before suffering a paralytic attack, and he died July 31, 1875.

Who was the only former President to serve in the House of Representatives after he left the White House?

John Quincy Adams. He served in the House of Representatives for almost 17 years, from March 1831 until his death in February 1848.

Who was the only Speaker of the House of Representatives to be elected President?

James K. Polk, who had been Speaker from 1835 to 1839.

Who was the only President defeated for reelection but later elected to a second term?

Grover Cleveland, who was elected to the presidency in 1884, defeated in 1888, and elected again in 1892.

Who was the first President to be censured by a house of Congress?

Andrew Jackson, in 1834. President Jackson bitterly opposed the Bank of the United States, and he removed federal deposits from the bank. This action prompted Henry Clay to introduce two resolutions censuring the President, and both passed in the Senate, by votes of 28 to 18 and 26 to 20. (The censure resolutions were stricken from the Senate records in 1837 because of the persistent pressure of Senator Thomas Hart Benton.)

How many Democratic Presidents served as governor of New York before they moved to the White House?

Three—Martin Van Buren, Grover Cleveland, and Franklin D. Roosevelt.

Who was the first President to be inaugurated in Washington, D.C.?

Thomas Jefferson, who walked the one block from his boardinghouse to the Capitol on March 4, 1801.

The journal kept by what future President gave historians the most information about what occurred at the Constitutional Convention in 1787?

James Madison's journal supplied the most thorough account of the Constitutional Convention. Reporters and the public were barred from the convention sessions, so Madison's careful notes were a great help in later determining what took place at the sessions.

Who was the first President to take the oath of office in an outdoor inauguration?

James Monroe, on March 4, 1817. Following an argument between senators and congressmen over the distribution of seats in the House of Representatives, it was decided to hold the ceremony on a platform built on the east portico of the Capitol.

Who was the first President inaugurated on January 20?

Franklin D. Roosevelt, who was inaugurated for his second term on January 20, 1937. The Twentieth ("Lame Duck") Amendment, ratified in February 1933, moved the inauguration date up from March 4 to January 20.

What President had served as United States minister to five different countries?

John Quincy Adams. He was named minister to the Netherlands in 1794, to Portugal in 1796, to Prussia in 1797, to Russia in 1809, and to England in 1815.

During what President's administration was the size of the United States almost doubled?

This occurred in 1803 during Thomas Jefferson's administration when the Louisiana Purchase was consummated. For $15 million Napoleon sold the United States all French lands from the Mississippi Delta to the Canadian border.

Who were the first two Presidents to leave Washington, D.C., without attending the inaugurations of their successors?

The two Adamses, father and son. John Adams refused to attend the inauguration of Thomas Jefferson, and John Quincy Adams shunned the inauguration of Andrew Jackson. Their bitter feelings can be partly explained because John Adams and his son John Quincy were the first two Presidents who failed to be reelected.

Which President was a splendid writer but a poor public speaker?

Thomas Jefferson. Because he was inept as an orator, Jefferson ended the tradition of delivering the President's annual messages to Congress in person. This tradition was not revived for more than a century, until Woodrow Wilson became President in 1913.

What was the most boisterous celebration in the history of presidential inaugurations?

Andrew Jackson's inaugural reception at the White House on March 4, 1829. Everyone was welcome, and some of Jackson's Western supporters turned the affair into a brawl. Many in the crowd got drunk, broke dishes and glasses, stood on chairs and sofas in their muddy boots, and overturned tables. Some even knocked each other to the floor when fistfights erupted.

Who was the chief architect of the Monroe Doctrine?

John Quincy Adams, who was Secretary of State in James Monroe's administration.

What future President was one of the three authors of *The Federalist Papers*, a series of essays that provided effective propaganda in the struggle to win ratification of the Constitution?

James Madison. The other two authors were Alexander Hamilton and John Jay.

Which future President went to Ghent, Belgium, as a member of the American delegation that negotiated the peace treaty ending the War of 1812?

John Quincy Adams.

What two-term President was saddened by the death of one Vice-President in his first term and another Vice-President in his second term?

James Madison. George Clinton, the Vice-President in Madison's first term, died in office on April 20, 1812. Elbridge Gerry, the Vice-President in Madison's second term, died in office on November 23, 1814.

What President sent Lewis and Clark on their two-year expedition that reached the Pacific Ocean?

Thomas Jefferson, who wanted to know more about the country west of the Mississippi River. To head the expedition, the President chose his young secretary, Captain Meriwether Lewis. Then Lewis invited his friend William Clark to share the leadership. They set out from St. Louis, Missouri, in May 1804, reached the Pacific Ocean near the mouth of the Columbia River in November 1805, and returned to St. Louis in September 1806.

Who was the only President to face enemy gunfire while in office?

James Madison, during the War of 1812. He assumed command of a battery stationed a half-mile north of Bladensburg, Maryland, in a futile attempt to prevent the capture of Washington, D.C., by the British.

What President had served as Secretary of State and Secretary of War at the same time?

James Monroe, who was Secretary of State from 1811 to 1817 and Secretary of War in 1814 and 1815.

What future President went to France to help Robert Livingston negotiate the Louisiana Purchase?

James Monroe.

What future President commanded the troops that defeated the British at New Orleans in a battle fought after the treaty ending the War of 1812 had been signed?

Andrew Jackson.

What Chief Executive died in the same room where he took the Presidential oath of office?

John Quincy Adams. He took the presidential oath of office in the Hall of the House of Representatives on March 4, 1825, and died in that room (while serving as congressman) on February 23, 1848.

Who was the only Vice-President besides Spiro Agnew to resign from that office?

John C. Calhoun, who was Vice-President during Andrew Jackson's first term as President, resigned in December 1832, to become a senator from South Carolina.

What President ordered the arrest of his former Vice-President for treason?

Thomas Jefferson ordered the arrest of Aaron Burr on treason charges in 1807, after Burr purportedly planned a conspiracy to take over Mexico and lead the Western territories out of the Union. President Jefferson was infuriated when his cousin but bitter political enemy Chief Justice John Marshall acquitted Burr because he said it could not be proven that the former Vice-President had committed an "overt act" against the United States.

Why did President Andrew Jackson refuse to carry out a decision rendered by the Chief Justice of the Supreme Court?

Andrew Jackson took the side of the state of Georgia in its dispute with the Cherokee Indians. When Chief Justice John Marshall handed down a judgment favoring the Cherokees, Jackson exclaimed, "John Marshall has made his decision. Now let him enforce it!"

What President set four goals for his administration, accomplished all of them, and then retired from the White House without seeking reelection?

James K. Polk. The four goals he set and achieved were acquiring California, settling the Oregon dispute with Great Britain, lowering the tariff, and establishing a subtreasury.

While he was military governor of Tennessee, what future President persuaded the legislature to end slavery and become the first Confederate state to return to the Union?

Andrew Johnson.

What Democratic President did not put his hand on a Bible when he took the oath of office?

Franklin Pierce, who refused to use a Bible at his inauguration because he felt that the recent death of his young son was a punishment for his sins. For the same reason, he said in his oath "I affirm," rather than "I swear."

What President had been a hangman who executed two convicted murderers?

Grover Cleveland, when he was sheriff of Erie County, New York, from 1871 to 1873.

What future President was intoxicated when he was sworn in as Vice-President?

Andrew Johnson, in 1861. He was still weak from a bout

with typhoid fever, so he took a large dose of liquor in the hope that it would make him feel stronger. During the inauguration ceremonies his gait was unsteady, and he slurred some of his words. Also, he talked at great length about his humble childhood and youth.

What Vice-President sometimes presided over the Senate wearing a pair of pistols because he feared the outbreak of violence?
Martin Van Buren.

What former President said, "I have no regret for any public act of my life, and history will vindicate my memory"?
James Buchanan said this shortly before his death in 1868. History, however, has not vindicated his memory. Buchanan is considered a weak President whose inaction and pro-Southern sympathies accelerated the coming of the Civil War.

What nickname was given to President Andrew Jackson's group of unofficial advisers?
The "Kitchen Cabinet."

Who was President when Alaska was purchased from Russia?
Andrew Johnson. In 1867 the United States purchased Alaska from Russia for $7.2 million.

Who was the only President to have served as a state senator, state attorney general, governor, United States senator, and Vice-President?
Martin Van Buren.

Who was the only President to stand trial on impeachment charges?
Andrew Johnson, in 1868. (Richard Nixon was indicted by the House of Representatives on impeachment charges in 1974, but he resigned from the presidency before the trial in the Senate began.)

By what vote margin was Johnson acquitted at his impeachment trial?
By one vote. A two-thirds vote of the Senate is required for conviction, and the Senate vote was guilty 35, not guilty 19.

What President said, "Public office is a public trust"?
Grover Cleveland.

To what situation did Franklin D. Roosevelt refer when he said, "The only thing we have to fear is fear itself"?
Roosevelt was referring to the severe economic problems created by the Great Depression when he made this statement in his inaugural address on March 4, 1933.

Who put on his White House desk a sign that read, "The buck stops here"?
Harry Truman.

In his inaugural address, what President said, "Ask not what your country can do for you—ask what you can do for your country"?
John F. Kennedy.

Who said, early in his presidency, "I do not think that I ever will get credit for anything I do—because I did not go to Harvard"?
Lyndon B. Johnson, who graduated in 1930 from Southwest Texas State Teachers College.

What President said, "If you can't stand the heat, stay out of the kitchen"?
Harry Truman.

Which President quoted the prophet Isaiah when he said, "Come now, and let us reason together"?
Lyndon B. Johnson.

Besides Franklin D. Roosevelt and his New Deal, other Democratic Presidents had names for their domestic programs. Whose programs were called the (a) New Freedom, (b) Fair Deal, (c) New Frontier, and (d) Great Society?
(a) Woodrow Wilson, (b) Harry Truman, (c) John F. Kennedy, and (d) Lyndon B. Johnson.

What President wanted to be called by his nickname even when he took the oath of office?
Jimmy Carter, who was baptized James Earl Carter, Jr.

Besides the presidency, did Franklin D. Roosevelt hold any other political offices that his cousin Theodore Roosevelt had held?

Yes, both Roosevelts served as Assistant Secretary of the Navy and as governor of New York. Also, both were members of the New York state legislature, Franklin as a senator and Theodore as an assemblyman.

What Chief Executive held the first presidential press conference?

Woodrow Wilson, on March 15, 1913.

Who made the first presidential address telecast from the White House?

Harry Truman, in 1947.

Who appointed the first Jewish justice of the Supreme Court?

Woodrow Wilson, who appointed Louis Brandeis to the Supreme Court on January 28, 1916.

What President appointed the first black to the Supreme Court?

Lyndon B. Johnson, who appointed Thurgood Marshall a Supreme Court justice in 1967.

What Vice-President mistakenly thought for about an hour that he had become President?

On November 23, 1919, several weeks after President Woodrow Wilson had suffered a paralytic stroke, Vice-President Thomas R. Marshall was speaking at a meeting in Atlanta when a policeman rushed to the podium and told Marshall that someone had just phoned and said the President had died. Visibly shaken, the Vice-President transmitted the sad news to the audience and said, "I cannot continue my speech. I must leave at once to take up my duties as Chief Executive of this great nation."

About an hour later Marshall learned that Wilson was still alive. (He did not die until 1924.) The Vice-President never discovered who had perpetrated this cruel hoax.

When he was a congressman, what future President tossed his expensive cowboy hat into the audience at political rallies?

Lyndon B. Johnson. But before each rally he would find a

young boy in the crowd and pay him a dollar to bring back the hat.

Did President Woodrow Wilson unveil his peace plan known as the Fourteen Points before or after the Armistice ending World War I?

Wilson announced his Fourteen Points in January 1918, many months before the Armistice, which occurred on November 11, 1918.

Following his inauguration, what President walked with his family the mile and a half from the Capitol to the White House?

Jimmy Carter, on January 20, 1977.

To promote the war effort, what President let a herd of sheep graze on the White House lawn?

Woodrow Wilson did this as a patriotic gesture during World War I. The sheep ate the grass, thus freeing some of the White House gardeners for war service. After the sheep were shorn, their wool was sold for about $100,000, which was donated to the Red Cross.

How did Harry Truman entertain Joseph Stalin and Winston Churchill at the Potsdam Conference in 1945?

By playing on the piano a beautiful rendition of Paderewski's "Minuet in G." Later, after Truman played the same piece at a Missouri county fair, he said to the audience, "When I played this, Stalin signed the Potsdam Agreement."

Who was the only Democratic President to win the Nobel Peace Prize?

Woodrow Wilson won this award for his role in creating the League of Nations following World War I.

In 1952 John F. Kennedy defeated what popular Republican to win a Senate seat from Massachusetts?

Henry Cabot Lodge, Jr. Exactly ten years later Kennedy's younger brother Edward defeated Lodge's son George for the same Senate seat.

What future President won the Democratic primary election for a Senate seat by 87 votes out of nearly one million votes that were cast?

In 1948 Lyndon B. Johnson won the Democratic Senate nomination in Texas over former Governor Coke R. Stevenson by a vote of 494,191 to 494,104. Charges of fraud erupted across the state, but a cursory investigation sustained the results. Johnson went on to defeat his Republican opponent easily in the final election.

After he became President unexpectedly, who told reporters that he felt as if "the moon, the stars, and all the planets had fallen on me"?

Harry Truman said this after he was elevated to the presidency by the sudden death of Franklin D. Roosevelt on April 12, 1945.

Which of these alphabet agencies or programs was not inaugurated during Franklin D. Roosevelt's New Deal: AAA, CCC, PWA, RFC, or WPA?

The RFC (Reconstruction Finance Corporation) was launched during Herbert Hoover's administration and continued under the New Deal.

What future President was first elected to the Senate with the help of the corrupt machine headed by Boss Tom Pendergast of Kansas City?

Harry Truman, in 1934.

What President appointed his own brother to his Cabinet?

John F. Kennedy named his brother Robert as his Attorney General.

What President had been minority leader of the Senate from 1953 to 1957 and Senate majority leader from 1957 to 1961?

Lyndon B. Johnson.

What Chief Executive dismissed General Douglas MacArthur as commander of the United Nations forces in the Korean War

because MacArthur failed to heed the President's orders?

Harry Truman, on April 11, 1951.

Who was President when the United States became involved in one episode in Cuba that was disastrous and another that was successful?

John F. Kennedy. The Bay of Pigs invasion in 1961 ended in disaster; the blockade of Soviet ships carrying missiles to Cuba in 1962 was successful.

What President appointed the first woman minister to a foreign country?

Franklin D. Roosevelt. On April 12, 1933, he appointed Ruth Bryan Owen, the eldest daughter of William Jennings Bryan, minister to Denmark.

In March 1965 President Lyndon B. Johnson sent the first 3,500 United States combat troops to Vietnam. By the end of 1968, how many American servicemen were in Vietnam?

More than 500,000.

What President appointed the first woman to his Cabinet?

Franklin D. Roosevelt appointed Frances Perkins Secretary of Labor in 1933.

Who was President when the first minimum wage law was passed?

Franklin D. Roosevelt. The Fair Labor Standards Act of 1938 set a minimum wage of 25 cents an hour for workers engaged in interstate commerce. As a result of this act, about 800,000 workers received immediate raises.

Was either Social Security or Medicare launched during the administration of Harry Truman?

No. The Social Security Act was passed in 1935 when Franklin D. Roosevelt was President, and Medicare was started in 1965 in Lyndon B. Johnson's administration. However, when Truman was President he had tried in vain to get Congress to approve Medicare. So after the measure was passed, Johnson flew to Independence, Missouri, to give Truman the pen he had used to sign the Medicare Act.

The historic Camp David Accord was facilitated by what President?

Jimmy Carter, who played a major role in bringing about this agreement between Egypt and Israel in September 1978.

What President appointed the first black to his Cabinet?

Lyndon B. Johnson appointed Robert C. Weaver Secretary of Housing and Urban Development in 1966.

Who was President during the Berlin Airlift when United States airplanes delivered food and fuel to the people of West Berlin for nearly a year?

Harry Truman.

What President created the Alliance for Progress and the Peace Corps to help people in underdeveloped countries?

John F. Kennedy.

How did Franklin D. Roosevelt's political enemies use his Scottie in an attack on the President?

They claimed that on a trip to the Pacific FDR left Fala, his Scottie, behind and sent a destroyer to bring the dog home. Roosevelt emphatically denied the charge.

Who was the only President sworn into office by a woman?

Lyndon B. Johnson, who was administered the presidential oath in Air Force One, following the assassination of President Kennedy, by United States District Judge Sarah Hughes.

What future President lost his primary race for a seat in the state senate, suspected election fraud, filed a challenge in the courts, and—three days before the general election—was declared the official Democratic nominee?

This happened to Jimmy Carter in 1963. He won the general election and served two terms in the Georgia state senate.

In what President's administration was the important nuclear-test-ban treaty signed by the United States and the Soviet Union?

This occurred on July 25, 1963, during the administration of President John F. Kennedy. The pact banned nuclear testing in the atmosphere, in outer space, and in the oceans, but not underground. By the end of the year 113 nations had indicated their willingness to support the treaty.

What Chief Executive appointed one Chief Justice of the Supreme Court and eight Associate Justices?

Franklin D. Roosevelt.

The most sweeping civil rights legislation was passed in the administration of what President?

Lyndon B. Johnson. While he was President, Congress passed laws ending racial discrimination in public accommodations, employment, and housing, and a law guaranteeing voting rights to Southern blacks.

Who was the first President to appoint three women to his Cabinet?

Jimmy Carter. He appointed Juanita Kreps Secretary of Commerce, Patricia Harris Secretary of Housing and Urban Development, and Shirley Hufstedler Secretary of Education.

What President sent Marines and other armed forces (totaling 23,000 servicemen) to the Dominican Republic because he said he feared a Communist takeover of that Caribbean country?

Lyndon B. Johnson did this in April 1965. The Communists did not seize the Dominican government, and about a month later patrols from the Organization of American States—including United States troops—took over peacekeeping duties.

What President stressed—more than any of his predecessors—the need to achieve human rights throughout the world?

Jimmy Carter.

Did any Democratic President ever reject a court subpoena?

Yes. In 1807 Chief Justice John Marshall issued a subpoena to President Thomas Jefferson to release a letter sought by defense attorneys in Aaron Burr's treason case. President Jefferson refused to comply with the subpoena, asserting that "the leading principle of our Constitution is the independence of the legislature, executive, and judiciary of each other. . . but would the executive be independent of the judiciary if he were subject to the commands of the latter and to imprisonment for dis-obedience?" The question of whether a President can be forced to comply with a subpoena was not tested in the Burr case because President Jefferson finally agreed to make most of the subpoenaed letters available to the court.

Another Democratic President, James Monroe, was sub-poenaed to testify at a court-martial. President Monroe refused to appear in court, but he answered written questions from the court.

What President pledged that the United States would land a man on the moon before the end of the decade?

John F. Kennedy made this pledge in 1961; Neil Armstrong and Edwin Aldrin walked on the surface of the moon in June 1969.

Who served longest as President?

Franklin D. Roosevelt, who was elected to four terms and served 4,422 days as Chief Executive. His record cannot be sur-passed because the Twenty-second Amendment, which went into effect in 1951, limits the President to two full terms.

The capital of an African country was named for what President?

Monrovia, Liberia, was named for James Monroe. During his administration Congress appropriated $100,000 to send freed slaves back to Africa, and in 1822 the American Colonization Society founded the republic of Liberia ("land of freedom") on the west coast of Africa as a haven for American blacks. During the next 38 years about 15,000 blacks moved from the United States to Liberia.

What President ordered that the following prayer, written by John Adams, be carved over the State Dining Room fireplace in the White House: "I pray heaven to bestow the best of blessings on this house and all that shall hereafter inhabit it. May none but honest and wise men ever rule under this roof"?

Franklin D. Roosevelt.

FIRST LADIES

How many former First Ladies were living in 1984?

Five: Jacqueline Kennedy, Lady Bird Johnson, Pat Nixon, Betty Ford, and Rosalynn Carter.

What First Lady established the White House as the social center of Washington?

Dolley Madison. She reinstated Abigail Adams's weekly levees and added Wednesday night "drawing room" parties. She also gave luncheons, teas, dinner parties, lawn parties, and fancy balls. Author Washington Irving loved his visits to the White House while Mrs. Madison reigned as the queen of Washington society.

Why did Dolley Madison serve as White House hostess during Thomas Jefferson's administration?

Widower Jefferson was the first President to live in the White House for his entire two terms. His married daughters did not care to be White House hostesses. Vice-President Burr was also a widower. Thus Mrs. Madison, wife of the Secretary of State, was the highest-ranking hostess in the capital. The Madisons lived in the White House as Jefferson's guests during their first few weeks in Washington, and Dolley Madison remained on call for the President's social functions.

But it was Mrs. Madison's charm that made her the idol of Washington. "She talks a great deal in such quick, beautiful tones. So polished and elegant are her manners that it is a pleasure to be in her company," said her portrait painter.

What First Lady had a major congressional bill named for her?

Lady Bird Johnson. The "Lady Bird Bill" was a significant highway beautification law that eliminated thousands of billboards and junk heaps along the nation's freeways and highways.

When she wed John F. Kennedy, Jacqueline Bouvier was given away by her stepfather, Hugh Auchincloss, even though her real father had led her down the church aisle at the rehearsal the day before. Why?

Her real father, John Bouvier III, did not appear at the church for the wedding.

Who was the only President to have two First Ladies?

Woodrow Wilson. When Ellen Axson Wilson, his wife of nearly 30 years, died in August 1914, the President was disconsolate. The following year Wilson's cousin introduced him to Edith Bolling Galt, a handsome widow. Mrs. Galt raised the President's spirits for the first time in months. They were married at her home in December 1915. The second Mrs. Wilson survived her husband by nearly 38 years, living until December 28, 1961. At the inauguration of John F. Kennedy in January 1961, Mrs. Wilson rode in the same car with Eleanor Roosevelt.

For 13 consecutive years the Gallup Poll recorded that what First Lady was the "most admired woman in the world"?

Eleanor Roosevelt. Upon her death in November 1962, the United Nations General Assembly members stood a moment in silent tribute. Secretary of State Dean Rusk remembered Mrs. Roosevelt in this way: "She had no capacity for hate, but much for indignation, which led to her passionate protests against disease, poverty, injustice, and prejudice."

How has the job of First Lady grown?

By 1980 Rosalynn Carter employed a record-high staff of

20 persons. Eleanor Roosevelt's staff 40 years earlier had been 3: an administrative secretary, a social secretary, and a messenger.

Mrs. Carter's schedule in her first two years as First Lady included 400 White House official social functions, 248 major speeches, 154 press interviews, 68 appearances at political events, 641 briefings attended, 36 countries visited, and 152 United States cities visited.

What First Lady in the 1840s banned liquor, card playing, and dancing from the White House?

Sarah Childress Polk, who greeted visitors from a seated position, usually dressed in somber-hued velvet.

How did Sarah Polk's role in the White House foreshadow the struggle for women's equality?

A woman of unusual intelligence and education, Mrs. Polk served in the official capacity of confidential secretary to her husband. No President had ever before employed a woman officially in the post.

What First Lady, who was called "the very picture of melancholy," wore black every day in the White House?

After the third and last of her sons had died in childhood, Jane Pierce took it as an omen that God had chosen her husband to be President and that his family was to be sacrificed for the sake of the presidency. She spent her White House years alone, often writing letters to her dead sons.

Why did Eleanor Roosevelt have a difficult childhood?

Though the family had wealth and prominence, young Eleanor's childhood was a torment. She was mocked as "odd" by her beautiful mother, who constantly bemoaned the fact that her daughter was not pretty. Intermittently, Eleanor's dashing, alcoholic father flooded her with affection, then ignored her.

After her parents died, when she was still a child, Eleanor was reared by a grim, strict grandmother who believed her to be ungainly and sent her off to boarding schools run by stern teachers.

Shy, insecure, and lonely, Eleanor in her adolescent years found debutante parties "an agony."

What First Lady bought a small radio station and watched it grow into a network of major broadcasting companies?

Lady Bird Johnson, who first invested in a radio station in Austin, Texas, in 1943.

What President and First Lady were hosts to a live alligator?

President and Mrs. John Quincy Adams. The alligator belonged to General Lafayette, the French hero of the American Revolution, who stayed in the White House all summer in 1825. His alligator lived in the East Room.

What First Lady claimed she was a direct descendant of Pocahontas?

Edith Bolling Galt, the second wife of Woodrow Wilson.

What future First Lady taught her husband reading, writing, and arithmetic?

Eliza McCardle Johnson, the wife of Andrew Johnson. She was the daughter of the local shoemaker and had received a good basic education, but her husband never had a chance to go to school.

Who held the first wedding in the White House?

President and Mrs. James Monroe hosted the wedding of their 16-year-old daughter Maria to Samuel L. Gouverneur at the White House in 1820.

What First Lady was hailed as "Ravissante! Charmante! Belle! Le Magnifique" in French newspaper headlines?

Jacqueline Bouvier Kennedy. Of French heritage, she had spent one college year studying at the Sorbonne and spoke and read French fluently.

John Kennedy opened his press conference in Paris by saying, "I do not think it altogether inappropriate to introduce myself to this audience. I am the man who accompanied Jacqueline Kennedy to Paris, and I have enjoyed it."

Over lunch at the Elysee Palace, President de Gaulle said to JFK, "Your wife knows more French history than any French woman."

Who was the youngest First Lady?

Frances Folsom, who at 21 married her late father's former law partner, President Grover Cleveland, who was 49. Cleveland was the only President to marry in the White House.

What First Lady had the longest life?

Bess Truman, who died at 97.

What Democratic First Lady had a Republican President give her away as bride at her wedding?

Eleanor Roosevelt. Her favorite "Uncle Ted" (President Theodore Roosevelt) served as "father of the bride" at her 1905 marriage to her distant cousin, future Democratic President Roosevelt.

Who was the first President's wife to remarry after her husband's death?

Frances Cleveland. She survived Grover Cleveland, who died in 1908, by nearly 40 years. Mrs. Cleveland married Thomas Preston, Jr., a professor of archaeology at Princeton University, in 1913.

Who was the only other First Lady to remarry after her husband's death?

Jacqueline Kennedy, who married Aristotle Onassis, a Greek millionaire, in 1968, almost five years after the death of John F. Kennedy.

"She's the girl I want to marry," said a future President to his mother after his first date with a 17-year-old girl. Who was he?

Jimmy Carter, who first dated his neighbor, Rosalynn Smith, when he was on leave from the U.S. Naval Academy in 1945, and Rosalynn was home from her first year at Georgia Southwestern College. She dropped out of college to marry Carter in 1946.

Who introduced Dolley Todd to her future husband, James Madison?

Aaron Burr.

What First Lady was courted by her husband on the golf links and later, as a new bride, golfed nearly every morning, even though she usually needed 200 strokes to finish the course?

Edith Wilson.

How did President Truman respond to his wife's failure to break the ceremonial champagne bottle at the dedication of the first hospital airplane?

He chuckled and told her she should have spat on her hands and let fly with the mighty swing he remembered from their childhood days playing sandlot baseball together. Bess Truman didn't enjoy his humor. "I'm sorry I didn't swing that bottle at you," she retorted.

Actually, the bottle had made two healthy dents in the airplane's aluminum fusilage under Mrs. Truman's blows. An alert mechanic saved the day by holding the bottle against the plane and smashing it with his wrench.

According to legend, during the War of 1812 Dolley Madison took down from the wall Gilbert Stuart's portrait of George Washington, so it would be saved from the British who were advancing on the White House. Did she really do this?

No. The portrait was too high for Mrs. Madison to reach, and it was tightly screwed to the wall. So the gardener climbed a ladder, broke the frame with an axe, and handed the valuable painting to the First Lady.

How did daily life in the White House change during World Wars I and II?

Edith Wilson kept her sewing machine busy, making garments for the wounded. The Wilsons also planted a vegetable garden and observed meatless and wheatless days.

During World War II the Roosevelts were kept busy greeting a continuous stream of Allied officials. Security measures at the White House were strict. Gun crews watched from the White House roof, blackout curtains hung at every window, and an underground shelter was built. Every resident had a gas mask; one hung from FDR's wheelchair at all times.

Who fainted when she learned that the Democrats had nominated her husband for the presidency?

Jane Pierce.

Who was the only son of a President and First Lady to be married in the White House?

John Adams, son of President and Mrs. John Quincy Adams, married his cousin Mary Catherine Hellen in 1828 in what was later called the Blue Room.

Why did President and Mrs. Jimmy Carter send their child Amy to a Washington, D.C., public school?

They enrolled nine-year-old Amy in a nearby public school to affirm their belief in racial integration and the quality of education in public schools.

What President and First Lady had four sons who served in the armed forces during World War II?

Franklin D. and Eleanor Roosevelt.

Who was the first child born to the wife of a President in the White House?

Esther Cleveland, born on September 9, 1893. She was the second child of President and Mrs. Grover Cleveland.

Which Democratic First Ladies in the twentieth century came from broken homes?

Both of Eleanor Roosevelt's parents died before she was 10. Bess Truman's father sat in a bathtub and killed himself with a pistol when Bess was 18. (No reason was ever given for his suicide.) Jacqueline Kennedy's parents were divorced when she was 13. Lady Bird Johnson's mother died when she was 5. Rosalynn Carter's father died when she was 13.

What bereaved First Lady personally informed the Vice-President that her husband had died?

Eleanor Roosevelt. In a touching conversation later described by the soon-to-be President, Harry Truman, Mrs. Roosevelt ended by asking him, "What can we do for you?"

What First Lady was called the "unofficial President" after her husband became incapacitated?

Edith Wilson. Her husband, Woodrow Wilson, had about 17 months to serve in his second term when he was paralyzed by a stroke. During this period of time Mrs. Wilson decided which issues were to be presented to the President and whom he would be allowed to see.

She was determined to protect her husband. A doctor had told her, "Always keep in mind that every time you take him a new anxiety or problem to excite him, you are turning a knife in an open wound."

Was Bess Truman often consulted about the problems her husband faced as President?

Yes. Harry Truman acknowledged that he never made a major decision without discussing it with his wife. "Her judgment was always good," he said. "She looks at things objectively, and I can't always."

After Dolley Madison's tenure, did the First Ladies continue to make the White House the social center of Washington?

Rarely. Elizabeth Monroe stunned and angered Washington wives by refusing to return any calls. Worse yet, she greeted vistiors from a raised platform, as if to remind them of their inferiority. Louisa Adams's graciousness was not enough to soften the stiffness of her husband, John Quincy Adams. The next two Presidents, Jackson and Van Buren, were widowers. For many years presidential wives were invalids (the first Mrs. Tyler, Mrs. Taylor, Mrs. Fillmore), grief-stricken recluses (Mrs. Pierce), or abstemious persons who did not enjoy parties (Mrs. Polk).

Who was the only First Lady born outside the United States?

Louisa Catherine Johnson Adams was born in London to an English mother and an American father. She came to the United States for the first time at age 26, four years after her marriage to diplomat John Quincy Adams, the future President.

Which First Lady wore elaborate turbans and offered guests a pinch from the ornate snuffbox she always carried?

Dolley Madison. With her constant round of dinners, receptions, levees, lawn parties, and returning calls, Mrs. Madison was adored by men and women alike. "Not until Jacqueline Kennedy's day," said one White House historian, "would an equally glamorous figure dominate the social scene in Washington."

What First Lady became world-famous for her constant travels and for meeting people in all walks of life?

Eleanor Roosevelt. In one *New Yorker* cartoon a dusty-faced coal miner in the bowels of the earth glances upward and says, "Oh my goodness, it's Mrs. Roosevelt!" During the 1930s her visits ranged from breadlines (where she ladled out soup), to prisons, to ceremonial occasions for prominent politicians. And, yes, she did go down into a coal mine.

What First Lady visited seven Latin American nations in one trip, as *official* representative of the President of the United States?

Rosalynn Carter, in 1977. Prior First Ladies had taken foreign trips, but Mrs. Carter was the first empowered to conduct policy discussions with heads of state.

What future First Lady may have prevented the execution of the wife of the Marquis de Lafayette?

Elizabeth Monroe, whose husband was the American minister to France during the French Revolution, when Madame Lafayette had been sentenced to die by the guillotine. Mrs. Monroe visited Madame Lafayette at the prison gate, and her public demonstration of sympathy for the ill-fated French woman may have been the reason government authorities later released Madame Lafayette.

Grover Cleveland was the only President to serve two nonconsecutive terms. How did Mrs. Cleveland respond to her husband's leaving office after one term?

Frances Cleveland said to a servant, "Now, Jerry, I want you to take good care of all the furniture and ornaments in the house. . . for I want to find everything just as it is now when we come back again. For we are coming back, just four years from today." She was right.

What former First Lady wrote the Universal Declaration of Human Rights and led the fight for its adoption by the United Nations?

Eleanor Roosevelt, who served as a United States delegate to the UN General Assembly in 1945, 1947-52, and 1961.

What First Lady was keenly interested in programs to help the mentally ill?

Rosalynn Carter.

What President and First Lady were so frugal that they saved about half of the $25,000-a-year presidential salary and retired comfortably on its proceeds?

Franklin and Jane Pierce.

Rosalynn Carter was called "an extension of myself" by her husband, President Jimmy Carter. What did he mean?

Rosalynn Carter became the President's closest confidante on national issues of substance, as well as his official representative at many government functions. She often attended Cabinet meetings and high-level briefings.

What First Lady went before the Democratic national convention to plead with the delegates to nominate the man her husband wanted as his running mate?

Eleanor Roosevelt did this in 1940 when many of the convention delegates were resisting her husband's choice of Henry Wallace as the vice-presidential nominee. Mrs. Roosevelt got her way.

What was Lady Bird Johnson's real first name?

Claudia. However, she was called Lady Bird from infancy.

What First Lady won first place in the shotput at a school track meet?

Bess Truman.

What First Lady held weekly press conferences and wrote a daily newspaper column—both "firsts" for a President's wife?

Eleanor Roosevelt, who first spoke in the White House to 46 newspaperwomen on March 6, 1933, two days after her husband's inauguration. Her column, "My Day," was carried by hundreds of newspapers, including some conservative dailies which castigated the New Deal.

What First Lady restored the White House with furnishings and art from the nation's past, and then showed its new appearance on television?

Jacqueline Kennedy. When she first moved into the White House, Mrs. Kennedy considered its furnishings to be historically anachronistic and mediocre in quality. So Mrs. Kennedy persuaded Congress to create a new National Arts Commission for the White House, which assisted her in collecting antiques that represented the finest examples of American craftsmanship and art.

"Everything in the White House must have a reason for being there," she insisted. "It would be a sacrilege merely to 're-decorate' it—a word I hate. It must be restored. . . .That is a question of scholarship."

When the restoration was completed, about 80 million persons watched "A Tour of the White House with Mrs. John F. Kennedy," a 60-minute TV documentary.

Which First Lady often carried a pistol in her pocketbook and another in her car's glove compartment?

Eleanor Roosevelt.

When she was young, what First Lady was proud of being the only girl in town who could whistle through her teeth?

Bess Truman.

How did Jacqueline Kennedy break her ankle when she was a new bride?

By playing touch football with the vigorous Kennedy clan. After this accident, Mrs. Kennedy permanently retired to the sidelines.

What First Lady and President invited a convicted murderer to live in the White House and care for their daughter?

Rosalynn and Jimmy Carter. Mary Fitzpatrick had worked for the Carters under a state prison work-release system when

Carter had been Georgia's governor. The Carter family believed in her innocence and grew to trust her, and Amy loved Mrs. Fitzpatrick. President and Mrs. Carter, who maintained that her conviction had been the result of injustice to poor black defendants in their state, invited her to the White House to live with them. Later, Georgia authorities granted Mrs. Fitzpatrick a full pardon.

Why did President and Mrs. Truman spend four years of his administration outside the White House?

When they had first moved to the Executive Mansion, the Trumans had noticed signs of disrepair. The President's bathtub was sinking into the floor, and one leg of daughter Margaret's piano went through the ceiling of a dining room below. Inspection by architects and engineers revealed that the building was ridden with structural weaknesses and fire hazards. The Commission of Public Buildings concluded that the family floor was staying in place "purely from habit."

Repairing the White House proved to be a major undertaking, and while the work was proceeding the Trumans lived in nearby Blair House. During the reconstruction only the exterior walls remained intact, and all panels, moldings, friezes, and fixtures that could be preserved were set aside and reinstalled in the new steel-beam-supported structure.

Who hostessed the first inaugural ball in Washington, D.C.?

Vivacious Dolley Madison. She was the belle of the ball, wearing a buff velvet gown with a long train and a buff velvet turban from Paris, trimmed with plumes and white satin.

CAMPAIGN TRAILS,

1796-1852

Who were the candidates in the election of 1796, the first contested presidential election?

The Federalists nominated Vice-President John Adams for the presidency and Thomas Pinckney of South Carolina for the vice-presidency. The Democratic-Republicans chose Thomas Jefferson for the presidency and Aaron Burr of New York as his running mate.

How had these candidates been selected?

By congressional caucuses. The Federalist members of Congress met at a party caucus to decide who would be their candidates. The Democratic-Republican members of Congress also held a caucus to name their candidates. Nominating conventions, which now select the candidates of political parties, were not introduced until the 1830s.

The Electoral College was established by the Constitution to elect the President and Vice-President. But in the early days of the republic there were not separate elections for these two offices. Why was this so?

The Founding Fathers had not anticipated the emergence of political parties. So in the Constitution they provided for a single group of candidates from which both the President and the Vice-President would be selected. The Constitution makers expected that the best candidate would get the most votes and become President and that the second best candidate would get the second highest number of votes and be elected Vice-President.

How were the electors selected?

The Constitution lets each state legislature decide how that state's electors are selected. In 1796 there were 16 states, and in 10 of them the electors were chosen by the legislatures. (In these 10 states the ordinary voter had no voice in the election of the President and Vice-President.) Only 6 states held elections by popular vote to select the presidential electors.

When did every state allow its citizens to vote directly for the electors?

Slowly the states, one by one, accepted this democratic practice of holding popular elections for presidential electors. By 1836 every state except one had come around to this idea. South Carolina, however, clung to the method of having its electors selected by the state legislature until 1868. Before that date the voters of South Carolina were denied the opportunity to participate directly in presidential elections!

How did Alexander Hamilton plan to deny the presidency to John Adams in 1796?

Hamilton and Adams both were Federalists, but the two men disliked each other intensely. Hamilton hoped that Thomas Pinckney, the Federalist candidate for the vice-presidency, would gain more electoral votes than Adams and thus emerge from the election as the new President. This could happen, Hamilton figured, if some of the Federalist electors gave one of their two votes to Pinckney but withheld their second vote from Adams. Some friends of Adams, however, learned of Hamilton's scheme and were determined to fight back. They decided to "split the ticket" and vote for Adams but not for Pinckney.

How did "splitting the ticket" affect the outcome of the 1796 election?

Adams, the Federalist, was elected President with 71 electoral votes, and Jefferson, the Democratic-Republican, was elected Vice-President with 68 electoral votes.

Was a sectional rift apparent in this election?

Yes. Adams carried New England, New York, New Jersey, Delaware, and the majority of Maryland's electors. Jefferson won the Southern states and Pennsylvania.

What was unusual about the 1796 election?

It was the first and only time in the history of presidential elections that the President and Vice-President were chosen from opposing tickets.

Who were the candidates in the 1800 election?

The Federalists' caucus nominated John Adams to run for reelection, and his running mate was Charles C. Pinckney of South Carolina (the brother of Thomas Pinckney). The Democratic-Republicans ran the same ticket they had nominated in 1796: Thomas Jefferson and Aaron Burr.

How did the Democratic-Republican electors prove their party loyalty in this election?

Each of them faithfully cast one of his two votes for Jefferson and the other for Burr, so the party's candidates for President and Vice-President tied with 73 votes apiece! John Adams, with 65 votes, was denied a second term as Chief Executive.

When Jefferson and Burr tied in the electoral vote, how was the winner selected?

According to the Constitution, the tie had to be broken by the House of Representatives. When the election went to the House, each state had one vote.

At that time which political party controlled the House of Representatives?

The Federalists still controlled the House, for it was a lame-duck House that had been elected in 1798. So, ironically, the Federalists had the key role in deciding which of the two Democratic-Republicans would be the next President.

Did any Federalists in the House want to elect Burr President?

Yes. Some Federalists hated Jefferson, the head of the opposition party, and they relished the prospect of denying him the presidency by electing Burr to that position. Also, Burr was considered the lesser evil because he was a Northerner (like most Federalists), a lawyer instead of a farmer, and a practical politician who might be more susceptible to compromise than the philosopher Jefferson.

Hamilton, however, did not go along with the scheme to send Burr to the White House. Although Jefferson had been his chief rival, Hamilton felt he would be a better President than Burr, who he thought was devoid of scruples and interested only in promoting his own career.

How many ballots were cast by the House of Representatives before Jefferson was elected President?

In the early balloting 8 of the 16 states voted for Jefferson and 6 for Burr; the representatives of Maryland and Vermont were equally divided, so these 2 states lost their votes. Jefferson needed only 1 more state to gain a majority of votes and the presidency, but for 35 ballots the supporters of Burr could not be budged. Finally, on the 36th ballot the impasse was broken when a few Federalists refrained from voting, and the election then went to the rightful candidate. The final tally showed Jefferson won 10 states, Burr won 4, and 2 were divided.

How was an electoral-vote tie between a party's presidential and vice-presidential candidates prevented in future elections?

Before the next election the Twelfth Amendment was added to the Constitution; it provided for separate elections for President and Vice-President.

In his inaugural address, how did Jefferson allay the fears of those Federalists who believed that the "Revolution of 1800" might lead to the destruction of the national government?

The election in 1800 of Jefferson and a Congress dominated by his political party marked the first time in our country's history when the power to govern had changed hands. Some Federalists were gravely concerned that the strong central government they had carefully nurtured might be torn asunder by the newly elected supporters of democracy and feared that the end result would be anarchy and chaos.

Jefferson, who had described the election results as a "revolution," was keenly aware of the Federalists' fears. So in his inaugural address he declared, "We are all Republicans, we are all Federalists." By this he meant that in spite of their distrust of centralized power, he and his followers did not propose to destroy the federal government and that, despite their distrust of democracy, the Federalists recognized the principle that government decisions are finally settled by the will of the people.

As an added testament to his belief that a democratic government is strong enough to withstand dissent, the new President concluded, "If there be any among us who would wish to dissolve this Union or to change its republican form, let them stand undisturbed as monuments of the safety with which error of opinion may be tolerated where reason is left free to combat it."

Did Jefferson have as much difficulty winning reelection in 1804 as he had in winning his first term in the White House?

No. By 1804 the Federalists' appeal to the voters had declined markedly. Their presidential candidate that year, Charles C. Pinckney, won only 14 electoral votes to Jefferson's 162.

Today a major criticism of presidential elections is that one candidate wins all of a state's electoral votes and the other wins none. One suggested reform is to split states' electoral votes by dividing each state into districts, and whichever candidate wins in a district would get that district's electoral vote. Was this procedure ever used in our presidential elections?

Yes. In early elections some states set up separate electoral districts. This is why, for example, in the election of 1804 Maryland gave Jefferson 9 electoral votes and Pinckney 2. Maryland followed this district procedure until 1832, longer than any other state. North Carolina, Illinois, Maine, and New York were other states that tried but later abandoned the district system. (Since 1972 Maine has selected 2 of its electors by the statewide vote and the other 2 electors on the basis of which party carried each of the state's 2 congressional districts.)

When Jefferson retired from the White House, was he pleased that the Democratic-Republican caucus in Congress had nominated James Madison to be his successor?

Yes. Secretary of State Madison was Jefferson's closest friend, and ever since the first days of the republic the two men had shared the leadership of the Democratic-Republican Party.

Did Madison win a landslide victory over his Federalist opponent in 1808?

Yes. Charles C. Pinckney again was the Federalist presidential candidate, and again he was badly beaten. Madison had 122 electoral votes to Pinckney's 47.

How did the War of 1812 affect the presidential campaign in 1812?

The United States went to war with England in June 1812, but large numbers of people in the maritime and commercial centers of New England and the middle Atlantic states bitterly opposed the war. They referred to it scornfully as "Mr. Madison's war" and vowed to drive Madison from the White House in the election that November.

What was unusual about the Federalist candidate for the presidency in 1812?

He was not a Federalist. Having no popular candidate in their own party, the Federalists nominated DeWitt Clinton, the Democratic-Republican governor of New York. They did this partly to break the "Virginia Dynasty" (Virginia had held the presidency since the birth of the nation except for Adams's one term) and partly because the Federalists believed Clinton was a peace advocate who, if elected, would end the war. Clinton, however, handled the war issue in an ambivalent manner, appealing for support from both those who wanted to wage it more vigorously and those who wanted to end the conflict.

In 1812, did Madison win reelection by a landslide?

No. The election was surprisingly close. To all of New England except Vermont, Clinton added New York, New Jersey, Delaware, and 5 of Maryland's 11 electoral votes. Madison carried Ohio, Vermont, and the entire South, but this would not have been enough to win the election. Pennsylvania was the key state. If Clinton had won it, he would have been the new President and probably would have ended the war with England. The vote in Pennsylvania was very close, but Madison won it by a narrow margin and was reelected with 128 electoral votes to Clinton's 89.

Did James Monroe have more trouble winning his party's nomination or the general election in 1816?

James Monroe received the Democratic-Republican nomination after a heated battle in his party's congressional caucus. Monroe captured 65 votes, and his rival for the nomination, William Crawford of Georgia, had 54 votes. Defeating his opposition in the general election was a much easier task for Monroe. The Federalists by this time were so weak that they did not even officially nominate a candidate. But the electors of Massachusetts, Connecticut, and Delaware—selected by the state legislatures—cast 34 votes for Federalist Rufus King, while Monroe amassed 183 electoral votes.

For a short period of time the United States had a one-party political system. How did this come about?

Following the War of 1812, an astonishing spirit of national unity spread across every section of the country. Americans everywhere were buoyed by such intense national pride and self-confidence that this period was called the "Era of Good Feelings." This strong surge of unity was expressed in politics, too. The long-declining Federalist Party had finally died, and for a few years no other party rose to fill its place. So when President Monroe ran for reelection in 1820 he faced no opposition. His election would have been unanimous except that one New Hampshire elector dissented and cast his vote for a fellow New Englander, John Quincy Adams.

Why did the system of nominating presidential candidates in congressional caucuses break down in 1824?

Several candidates, all Democratic-Republicans, entered the presidential race of 1824. Since only one presidential nominee could be selected by the congressional caucus, some of the candidates circumvented the caucus and were nominated by state legislatures. Henry Clay was the candidate of Kentucky, Andrew Jackson was nominated by Tennessee, and John Quincy Adams was the choice of Massachusetts and other New England states. However, Secretary of the Treasury William H. Crawford of Georgia was considered the front-runner in the early stages of the election. But Crawford's campaign was handicapped because he suffered a paralytic stroke in 1823. Also, nearly all of his support came from the Southern planters along the Atlantic seaboard.

The congressional caucus made Crawford the official nominee, but most of the senators and congressmen boycotted the caucus. Of the 216 Democratic-Republican members of the Senate and House, only 66 attended the caucus and 64 voted for Crawford. The other candidates immediately denounced "King Caucus" as an undemocratic and archaic institution.

So the system of nominating candidates by a congressional caucus died with the election of 1824. In 1828 the state legislatures endorsed candidates.

What happened in the 1824 election when four candidates, all from the same party, competed?

When the electoral votes were counted Jackson had 99, Adams 84, Crawford 41, and Clay 37. Jackson also led in the popular vote by a margin of nearly 40,000 over Adams, his nearest rival.

Nevertheless, Jackson had not won a majority of the electoral vote, so the election had to be decided by the House of Representatives. According to the Twelfth Amendment, the names of only the top three candidates—Jackson, Adams, and Crawford—were placed before the House. So Clay was eliminated from the race, but as the powerful Speaker of the House he wielded enormous influence, and Clay's support was crucial to the fate of the three contenders.

To whom did Henry Clay throw his support when the House of Representatives had to elect the President?

Clay and Jackson had been bitter political foes for many years. On the other hand, Clay respected the ability and integrity of Adams. So the congressman from Kentucky favored Adams and urged his friends in the House to vote for him.

How did a scrap of paper on the floor affect the election?

The vote in the House of Representatives was extremely close. Adams was sure of the votes of the 6 New England states, and, with the help of Clay, he carried Maryland, Ohio, Kentucky, Illinois, Missouri, and Louisiana. That gave him 12 of the 24 states, but he needed 1 more to win. New York was the key state, but its delegation in the House was badly divided. Adams was apparently the choice of 17 of the 34 House members from New York. However, unless the New Englander could pick up another supporter in the New York delegation, that state would abstain when the roll of the states was called, and Adams would be 1 vote short of victory.

As the vote of New York was about to be taken, one of the state's undecided House members, General Stephen Van Rensselaer, bowed his head in prayer for divine guidance. When he opened his eyes, Van Rensselaer noticed on the floor in front of him a scrap of paper. It was a ballot someone had dropped with the name of John Quincy Adams written on it. Van Rensselaer felt that God had spoken. He picked up the ballot and put it in the ballot box. Thus New York cast 18 of its 34 votes for Adams and paved the way for the son of a former President to be elected by capturing 13 of the 24 states. But Adams had been very lucky in other states besides New York. A change of 1 vote in 5 of the other 12 states Adams carried would have cost him their support.

Why did their political enemies charge that Adams and Clay had made a "corrupt bargain"?

Adams chose Clay as his Secretary of State, a logical appointment because the two men shared the same views on foreign affairs. But their enemies emphatically claimed that Adams had promised this important position to Clay if he would swing votes to the New Englander in the House of Representatives in the 1824 election. However, no reliable evidence in support of this charge has ever been found.

What was unique about the results of the 1824 election?

Andrew Jackson was the only candidate in our political history to win more electoral votes than any of his opponents but fail to gain the presidency. Jackson also led in the popular vote, but there were two other presidential elections (1876 and 1888) when the popular-vote winner was not elected because his opponent had more electoral votes.

It is no wonder that Jackson's supporters cried foul, stymied Adams's administration by blocking most of his measures in Congress, and plotted to get revenge in the next presidential election.

Did the Jacksonians gain their revenge in 1828?

Yes. Jackson won a huge victory, capturing 178 electoral votes to 83 for the incumbent Adams. Only New England, New Jersey, Delaware, and some of the electors in Maryland and New York supported the President's bid for a second term. Jackson swept all of the Southern and Western states. In this election the followers of Adams called themselves National Republicans, while the Jacksonians were called Democratic-Republicans, or simply Democrats.

Why was Andrew Jackson popular with many voters in the lower economic classes?

Although no longer a common man himself, Andrew Jackson became the symbol of the common people. Coming from a humble family, Jackson had had no formal schooling and had risen to wealth and prominence largely through his own efforts. He was the first President not to come from an aristocratic family and the first example of what was to become the cherished presidential success story—"from log cabin to White House." Jackson also fit the role of a military hero, an attribute that has appealed to large numbers of voters in many subsequent presidential elections. Moreover, Jackson—the first President from a frontier state west of the Atlantic seaboard—generally championed causes advocated by many small Western farmers.

How did Jacksonian democracy differ from Jeffersonian democracy?

Jeffersonian democracy was led by liberal-minded aristocrats, such as Jefferson and Madison, who believed that voting and officeholding should be limited to free white men who possessed some property or earned a specified income.

Jacksonian democracy, on the other hand, involved participation in the government by many more people. By the time of

Jackson's presidency, most states had dropped property qualifications for voting and officeholding, accepting the idea that
any white male was qualified to vote and to hold office. Also,
most of the states had transferred the power to select presidential
electors from the legislatures to the voters. Moreover, soon the
candidates for the two highest offices in the land would be
selected by national party conventions, a device regarded as
more democratic than naming the nominees by caucuses or
state legislatures.

Did the Democrats hold the first national nominating convention?

No. The first national nominating convention was held in
September 1831 by the Anti-Masonic Party. This small, short-
lived political party attracted mainly poor farmers and laborers
who resented the Masons, a secret fraternal organization that in
the 1830s appealed primarily to the upper economic classes.
The first Anti-Masonic convention was held in Baltimore, Maryland, and consisted of 116 delegates from 13 states. It nominated
former Attorney General William Wirt of Maryland to run in the
1832 presidential election.

Wirt, however, won less than 8 percent of the popular vote
and carried just one state, Vermont. This was the only presidential race in which the Anti-Masons ran a separate candidate,
and their influence declined sharply after the 1832 election.

What party held the second national nominating convention?

In December 1831 the National Republicans held their
convention in Baltimore. The bond that held this loosely
organized party together was their opposition to President
Jackson and his policies. Henry Clay was the convention's
unanimous choice to run for the presidency. No formal platform
was adopted, but the convention did endorse a strong statement
rebuking the actions of Jackson.

Did the first Democratic convention actually nominate Jackson to run for a second term?

No, because Jackson had already been nominated for reelection by various state legislatures, the national convention
simply approved the states' actions. But this first Democratic
national convention, held in Baltimore in May 1832, did select a
candidate for the vice-presidency. Following Jackson's request,

it named Martin Van Buren of New York as the President's running mate. While no official platform was adopted, each state delegation was asked to write its own statement about the major issues and then disseminate this report among the voters.

What rule was adopted by this first Democratic convention that made it difficult to nominate presidential candidates in many subsequent elections?

A two-thirds majority of delegate votes was required for the nomination of a candidate. This rule plagued many later Democratic conventions, which had to have numerous roll calls before any candidate received the votes of two-thirds of the delegates. Sometimes this led to deadlocks that could be broken only by giving the nomination to a compromise candidate.

The modern Republican Party never faced this problem because its conventions have always nominated candidates by a simple majority of votes (50 percent plus one). Finally, in 1936, the Democrats dropped the two-thirds rule and selected their nominees by a simple majority vote of the convention delegates.

Jackson had soundly defeated Adams when he won a first term in the White House in 1828. Did he do better or worse against Clay in 1832?

Jackson won the presidency by an even larger margin in the 1832 election. In 1828 he had 178 electoral votes; in 1832 he had 219 electoral votes. Clay carried only 5 of the 24 states, plus 5 of the 10 electoral votes of Maryland.

Why did the Democrats convene their second national convention in May 1835, almost 18 months before the next presidential election?

President Jackson wanted an early convention so that it could nominate his hand-picked successor before any opposition developed. The convention dutifully cast a unanimous vote for the President's choice, Vice-President Martin Van Buren.

What new major political party appeared on the political horizon in the 1836 election?

The Whigs. This new political party, which eventually sent four Presidents to the White House (two by election and two by elevation from the vice-presidency), was composed of the remnants of the Adams-Clay National Republican Party, the opponents of Jackson within the Democratic Party, and some members of the defunct Anti-Masonic Party. The members of this new party had one thing in common—hatred of Andrew Jackson, whom they called "King Andrew." They took the name "Whig" because it had been used in the American Revolution by those who opposed the King's tyranny.

The Whigs did not hold a national nominating convention in 1836. Instead, they ran regional candidates nominated by state legislatures. They knew that these various candidates would split the Whig vote, but their strategy was to keep enough electoral votes from Van Buren to send the election into the House of Representatives, where they could then unite behind the leading Whig candidate. Senator Daniel Webster of Massachusetts became New England's candidate; Senator Hugh L. White of Tennessee was the South's nominee; General William Henry Harrison of Ohio was the Whigs' chief contender in the rest of the country.

Did the Whigs' scheme to throw the 1836 election into the House of Representatives succeed?

No. Van Buren won handily with 170 of the 294 electoral votes. Harrison ran the best race of the three Whig candidates, gaining 73 electoral votes and 7 of the 26 states. Webster carried only Massachusetts, and White captured 2 states, Tennessee and Georgia. Although Jackson's heir apparent swept to a big victory, he didn't carry Tennessee, the home state of his benefactor.

Since the time when Jackson handed the White House keys to Van Buren, how many Presidents completed their terms of office and then were succeeded by their Vice-Presidents?

None.

What was unusual about the election of the Vice-President in 1836?

It was the only time in our political history when the Senate had to elect the Vice-President. (When no vice-presidential candidate wins a majority of the electoral vote, the election is thrown into the Senate.)

The Democratic candidate for Vice-President in 1836 was Richard M. Johnson of Kentucky. Johnson, the reputed slayer of the Indian chief Tecumseh, had lived with a mulatto woman by whom he had two children. This social behavior aroused much criticism, especially in the South. As a result, Johnson won the Democratic nomination for the vice-presidency by only 1 vote, and in the general election he received only 147 electoral votes—1 less than a majority. The runner-up in the election for Vice-President was the Whig candidate, Francis Granger of New York.

So the names of Johnson and Granger were submitted to the Senate, where each senator had 1 vote. The Senate elected Johnson Vice-President by a margin of 33 votes to Granger's 16.

When did the Whigs hold their first national convention?

In December 1839 at Harrisburg, Pennsylvania. Henry Clay wanted the 1840 presidential nomination, and he led on the first ballot. But General William Henry Harrison of Ohio won the nomination, and to give the ticket geographic balance John Tyler of Virginia was selected as Harrison's running mate.

Clay, sensing that the Whigs could win the White House in 1840, was bitter about losing the party's nomination. "It is a diabolic intrigue, I know now," he said, "which has betrayed me. I am the most unfortunate man in the history of parties: always run by my friends when sure to be defeated, and now betrayed for a nomination when I, or any one, would be sure of an election."

The Whigs were so divided on important issues that they did not even try to write a platform. Nor did they want nominee Harrison to make any promises. "Let him," said Nicholas Biddle, "say not one single word about his principles, or his creed—let him say nothing—promise nothing. Let no committee, no convention, no town meeting ever extract from him a single word about what he thinks nor what he will do hereafter. Let the use of pen and ink be wholly forbidden."

How did William Henry Harrison become the Tippecanoe part of the famous Whig slogan "Tippecanoe and Tyler too"?

In November 1811 General Harrison, advancing with 1,000 soldiers into Indian land, had suppressed a surprise Indian attack at Tippecanoe, in what is now Indiana.

In 1840 did the Democrats nominate Van Buren for a second term?

Van Buren lacked the charismatic appeal of Andrew Jackson, and during his administration the country suffered a severe depression. Nevertheless, the Democratic convention approved Van Buren's bid for another term in the White House. But Vice-President Richard M. Johnson was not renominated. Rumors circulated that Johnson was having affairs with other black women, so the convention decided to let state Democratic leaders determine who would run as the vice-presidential candidate in their own states.

The convention of 1840 produced the first Democratic Party platform, but it was a short statement, less than 1,000 words in length.

How did a disparaging remark about Harrison by a Democratic newspaper editor boomerang to help the Whig candidate?

The editor stupidly sneered at Harrison as a poor old farmer who would be content with a pension, a log cabin, and a barrel of hard cider. But instead of hurting Harrison's candidacy, this intended insult boosted his chances. Large numbers of Westerners lived in log cabins and drank hard cider; they could identify with a candidate who did the same. (Actually, Harrison came from a wealthy family, lived in a 16-room mansion, and did not drink hard cider.) The "log cabin, hard cider" image caught on with the public, and the Whigs stressed it again and again. Numerous torchlight parades featured banners and floats adorned with replicas of log cabins and cider barrels.

To draw a sharp contrast between their "homespun" candidate and the incumbent President, the Whigs portrayed Van Buren as an effete dandy who wore corsets, perfumed his whiskers, and ate French food with golden spoons from golden plates.

Was the presidential election of 1840 close?

In the popular vote, yes; in the electoral vote, no. Harrison narrowly defeated Van Buren in the popular vote 1,275,390 to 1,128,854. But the Whig candidate won the electoral count by a whopping 234 votes to 60. Van Buren captured only 7 of the 26 states and was humiliated when he did not even carry his home state of New York.

But after winning their first national election, the Whigs' euphoria did not last long. William Henry Harrison (at 68 the oldest President to enter the White House until Ronald Reagan's inauguration in 1981) died exactly one month after he was sworn into office. When Vice-President John Tyler, a former Democrat, assumed the presidency, he disagreed with the policies of the Whig leaders, and all of Harrison's Cabinet except Secretary of State Daniel Webster resigned.

Who was the first front-running Democrat to be denied the presidential nomination because he failed to win two-thirds of the convention votes?

Former President Martin Van Buren, in 1844. Van Buren was a strong favorite to win the nomination, but on the eve of the convention he issued a statement against the annexation of Texas, and this cost him the votes of many Southern delegates.

Even so, Van Buren received a simple majority of the votes on the first ballot. On later roll calls, however, his chief rival, Lewis Cass of Michigan, gained on Van Buren and eventually overtook him. But neither Cass nor Van Buren could get the 178 votes needed for nomination, and a stalemate developed.

Who was the first dark horse candidate to be nominated for President?

James K. Polk of Tennessee. (A dark horse candidate is an unexpected winner.) Polk was not even considered a presidential candidate when the 1844 convention began voting for its nominee, and he did not get a single vote during the first seven ballots. But the deadlock between Cass and Van Buren persisted, so the convention delegates finally turned to Polk as a compromise choice, and he won the nomination on the ninth ballot.

Before this occurred, Polk's political career had been going downhill. He had been governor of Tennessee from 1839 to 1841, but twice he had tried to be elected for a second term (in 1841 and 1843), and both times he was defeated.

What Democrat won the vice-presidential nomination in 1844 but refused to accept it?

Senator Silas Wright of New York. After he had been selected to run for Vice-President, Wright notified the convention that he would not accept the nomination. The convention then named George M. Dallas of Pennsylvania as Polk's running mate.

Did the Whigs run President Tyler for a second term in 1844?

No. The party leaders had battled with the President during his entire administration. When the Whigs refused even to consider him as a candidate at their 1844 convention, Tyler became the first President not to be nominated by his party for a second term. (The embittered Whig President supported the Democrat Polk in the election.)

In 1844 the Whigs nominated Henry Clay of Kentucky as their presidential nominee and Theodore Frelinghuysen of New Jersey as their vice-presidential nominee.

What third party entered a candidate in the presidential race in 1844?

In the 1840s the desire to end slavery was gaining much attention in American politics, and some abolitionists who felt that both major parties were weak on this issue started the Liberty Party. This third party had run James G. Birney of Michigan as their presidential candidate in 1840, but he polled less than 7,000 votes. In 1844 the Liberty Party again nominated Birney for the presidency.

Henry Clay was a three-time loser in the presidential sweepstakes. Did he ever come close to reaching the White House?

Yes, in 1844 Clay lost the presidency to James K. Polk by a razor-thin margin. Clay received 48.08 percent and Polk 49.54 percent of the popular vote. The key state in the election was New York. If Clay had won New York, he would have been elected President by an electoral-vote margin of 141 to 134. But Polk captured New York and with it the White House. However, Polk carried New York by only 5,106 votes out of nearly half a million ballots cast in that state.

Did the votes for Birney, the Liberty Party candidate, affect the outcome of the 1844 election?

Yes. James G. Birney got 15,812 votes in New York. Nearly all of these votes probably would have gone to Clay (whom most abolitionists preferred to Polk) if Birney had not been in the race. In fact, Clay could have won New York and the election by picking up less than one-third of Birney's votes in that state.

Birney ran a much stronger race in 1844 than he had run four years before. His 1844 vote totaled 62,103, more than nine times the number of votes he had won in 1840.

How did Polk learn that he had won the election?

News of election returns traveled slowly in those times. For days Polk did not know whether he had been elected. Then the postmaster at Nashville, Tennessee, opened a mail bag that had come from Cincinnati, Ohio. He noticed a penciled note from the Cincinnati postmaster. It said that Polk had carried New York and won the election. So the Nashville postmaster wrote this in a letter to Polk and had a messenger carry the letter to Polk's home in Columbia, 40 miles away. Changing horses, the messenger rode all night and reached Polk's home at dawn.

Whom did the Democrats nominate for President in 1848?

President Polk declined to run for a second term, so the race for the Democratic presidential nomination was wide open. On the fourth ballot the convention selected Senator Lewis Cass of Michigan. Cass was regarded as a "doughface," a term applied to Northerners who were sympathetic to the South's position on slavery.

The Whigs gave their presidential nomination in 1848 to a hero from the Mexican War. Who was he?

General Zachary Taylor, a Louisiana slaveholder who had never voted. (Taylor's daughter Sarah was married to Jefferson Davis, who became president of the Confederacy shortly before the Civil War began.) To balance the ticket with a Northerner, the Whigs selected Millard Fillmore of New York as Taylor's running mate.

The Free Soil Party was a new third party in the 1848 election. How did it differ from the older Liberty Party?

Although members of the old Liberty Party helped form a Free Soil Party, the new party was milder on the slavery issue than its predecessor. The Free Soilers did not press for the elimination of slavery in the Southern states but opposed its extension into the territories west of the Mississippi River that had not yet become states.

What former President was the Free Soilers' nominee to return to the White House?

Martin Van Buren.

What son of a former President did the Free Soilers nominate for the vice-presidency?

Charles Francis Adams of Massachusetts, the son of John Quincy Adams. (Later, from 1859 to 1861, Adams served in the House of Representatives.)

Taylor and Cass each won 15 states in the 1848 election. Was the election very close in the popular vote and the electoral vote?

No. Taylor had 47 percent of the popular vote to 42 percent for Cass. Taylor's margin of victory in the electoral vote was 163 to 127. Even though both candidates carried the same number of states, Taylor won a decisive victory because he captured New York and Pennsylvania, the two states with the largest population and the most electoral votes.

How did ex-President Van Buren, the Free Soil candidate, fare in the 1848 election?

While he did not carry a single state, Van Buren ran a stronger race than any other third-party candidate in previous presidential races. He won nearly 300,000 votes, which was more than 10 percent of the total popular vote.

In 1852 the Democrats named their second dark horse presidential nominee. Who was he?

Franklin Pierce of New Hampshire, who was selected as a compromise candidate on the 49th ballot. Pierce had served in both houses of Congress, but he had resigned from the Senate in 1842 to practice law and was not widely known throughout the country. His vice-presidential running mate was Senator William R. King of Alabama.

The Whig convention in 1852 took 53 ballots to select its presidential nominee. Who was he?

General Winfield Scott of Virginia, who had gained fame in the Mexican War as the conqueror of Mexico City.

Was the election of 1852 close?

No. The Democrat Pierce won by a landslide. He gained 254 electoral votes and carried 26 of the 30 states. Scott won in only 4 states with 42 electoral votes. John P. Hale, the Free Soil candidate, also did poorly, polling less than 5 percent of the total vote.

Did the weak showing of the Whigs and the Free Soilers in the 1852 election foretell the eclipse of these two political parties?

Yes. After 1852 both of these parties faded quickly from the political scene. But a new party was about to be born, and it would provide the Democrats with their strongest competition from 1856 to the present time.

CAMPAIGN TRAILS, 1856-1916

What act of Congress led to the founding of the Republican Party?

The Kansas-Nebraska Act of 1854 permitted settlers in these two territories to vote on whether they wanted slavery. This new legislation nullified the Missouri Compromise of 1820, which had forbidden slavery north of 36°30' latitude. Slave owners now could take over land that the Missouri Compromise had promised would forever be "free soil."

Antislavery leaders were infuriated by the Kansas-Nebraska Act, which triggered the creation of the Republican Party to fight the extension of slavery into the territories.

What groups of people came together to start the new party?

Northern Whigs, Free Soilers, abolitionists, and some antislavery Democrats joined to form the Republican Party.

When and where was the Republican Party born?

It is generally believed that the party's founders held their first meeting on February 28, 1854, at a church in Ripon, Wisconsin. The Republicans' first state convention was held in July 1854 in an oak grove outside the town of Jackson, Michigan.

Who was the first Republican nominee for the presidency?

The Republican convention in 1856 selected as its first presidential nominee John Charles Fremont, who had won fame as an explorer, an army officer in the Mexican War, and one of California's first senators. He ran on a platform strongly denouncing the spread of slavery into those areas in the United States that had not yet become states.

Why was it unusual that the Democrats selected Cincinnati, Ohio, as the site of their 1856 convention?

All of the six previous Democratic national conventions had been held in Baltimore, Maryland.

Did the Democrats nominate President Franklin Pierce to run for a second term?

No, Pierce had been a weak President, and the Democratic convention bypassed him in favor of James Buchanan of Pennsylvania. At a time when the slavery question was dividing the Democratic Party into Southern and Northern wings, Buchanan had an advantage over other candidates because he had been abroad the past three years as minister to Great Britain and was not deeply embroiled in the slavery issue. Even so, there were 17 roll calls before Buchanan won the nomination.

What Democrat felt he was too young to run for the vice-presidency?

John C. Breckinridge of Kentucky. Before the vice-presidential balloting started at the 1856 convention, Breckinridge asked to have his name withdrawn from consideration because he thought he was too young for the position. He was 35 (the youngest legal age to be a Vice-President) and declared that "promotion should follow seniority." The convention delegates disagreed and nominated Breckinridge anyway.

The "Know-Nothing" Party ran former President Millard Fillmore as its presidential nominee in 1856. What was this party, and how well did it do in the election?

The "Know-Nothing" Party (officially called the American Party) was a nativist political organization committed to placing restrictions on the millions of European immigrants who arrived in the 1840s and 1850s. The name "Know-Nothing" referred to the party members' extreme secretiveness. Andrew Jackson Donelson, who was the husband of Andrew Jackson's niece, was Fillmore's running mate on the "Know-Nothing" ticket.

Fillmore and Donelson also were endorsed by the nearly extinct Whig Party when it held its last convention in 1856.

The "Know-Nothings" set a new record for third-party entrants in a presidential race. Although Fillmore captured only one state, Maryland, he received 873,053 votes, which was over 21 percent of the popular vote. However, the "Know-Nothing" Party was a short-lived phenomenon that disappeared from the national political scene after 1856.

Why didn't Frémont win a single vote in ten Southern states?

The Republican Party—with its strong stand against the spread of slavery—was a sectional party in 1856, and the name of its presidential nominee did not even appear on the ballots of ten Southern states. In four other border states where slavery was allowed, Frémont's name was on the ballot, but he won only about 300 votes in each of these slave states.

Outside of the South and the border states, did Frémont run a strong race as the Republicans' first presidential nominee?

Yes. Democrat James Buchanan won the election, but Frémont captured 11 of the 15 states in the North and Midwest, including the large states of New York, Massachusetts, and Ohio.

(Beginning with the election of 1856, when the exciting rivalry between the modern Republican and Democratic parties was launched, the results of each presidential election are discussed in later chapters titled "Landslide Victories," "Cliff-Hangers," "Near Misses," and "Debacles." For more information about the 1856 election results, see pages 159 and 160.)

What was unique about the Democratic convention in 1860?

It was the only time that a major party adjourned its convention without nominating a presidential candidate and moved the convention from one city to another.

The convention first assembled in April 1860 in Charleston, South Carolina. Tempers soon flared when conflicting planks about the inflammatory slavery question were submitted for the party platform. The Southerners insisted that neither Congress nor any territorial legislature could interfere with slavery in the territories. Northern delegates favored Illinois Senator Stephen Douglas's popular sovereignty proposal, whereby the settlers in a territory would decide whether they wanted slavery, and they felt that only the Supreme Court could override the decision of the local settlers. When the convention voted to accept the milder approach of the Northerners, many Southern delegates walked out.

The remaining delegates then voted for a presidential nominee, and Senator Douglas led the field, but he could not win the necessary two-thirds majority of all the votes because the absent Southerners were still considered official members of the convention. After 57 roll calls it was obvious that no one could be nominated, so the convention was adjourned. Party leaders decided to meet again in June in the more neutral city of Baltimore, Maryland. In the meantime they hoped to patch up their differences with the Southern delegates.

Was harmony achieved at the reconvened convention in Baltimore?

No. The same rift between Northerners and Southerners recurred, and some delegates from the slave states walked out again. But this time Senator Douglas won the presidential nomination when the convention changed the rule so that he needed only a two-thirds majority vote of the delegates present.

What did the Southern delegates do after they bolted the Baltimore convention?

They held their own convention at Richmond, Virginia, where they nominated Vice-President John C. Breckinridge of Kentucky for the presidency and adopted a platform which stated that no branch of the government could outlaw slavery in the territories.

Before the Republican convention met in 1860, was Abraham Lincoln favored to win the Republican nomination?

No. Most politicians thought that the nomination would go to New York Senator William H. Seward. However, because of his radical antislavery stand, Seward had made numerous enemies in the party. Lincoln was one of several favorite-son candidates, but he had an advantage over some of the others because he had made few enemies. Also, another reason the rail splitter from Illinois won the nomination was that the Republican chieftains believed he would run strongly in the Midwestern states, which the Republicans needed to win the election.

How did the campaigns of Lincoln and Douglas differ?

Lincoln followed the tradition of most nineteenth-century presidential candidates—he stayed at home during the entire campaign. He made speeches, wrote newspaper articles, answered letters, and shook hands with many visitors who came to Springfield to meet him.

Douglas, on the other hand, was one of the first presidential nominees to take his campaign on the road. Douglas made speeches from New York west to Missouri, and when he traveled into the unfriendly South he gallantly stressed that the slave states should not secede from the Union, regardless who won the election.

In spite of Douglas's active campaigning, Lincoln became the first Republican elected to the presidency. (See pages 170 and 171 for the 1860 election results.)

In the 1864 election, why did the Republican Party use a different name and nominate a Democrat for the vice-presidency?

During the Civil War the Republican Party wanted to broaden its base by appealing to Democrats, as well as Republicans, who supported the Union cause. So in 1864 the party was called the Union Party, and Andrew Johnson of Tennessee, a War Democrat who had stayed loyal to the United States even after his own state had seceded, was selected as Lincoln's running mate.

Who was Lincoln's Democratic opponent in the 1864 election?

Union General George B. McClellan, the former commander of the Army of the Potomac, was the Democratic presidential nominee. Lincoln had feuded with McClellan about military strategy and removed him from his command, so the general had a personal grudge to settle with the President.

General McClellan refused to support the most important plank in the Democratic Party platform. Why was this so?

The Democratic platform, written by the peace faction of the party, called for an immediate end to the Civil War without victory for either side. General McClellan repudiated this plank in the platform. "I could not look in the faces of my gallant comrades of the army and navy who have survived so many bloody battles," he declared, "and tell them that their labors and the sacrifices of so many of our slain and wounded brethren had been in vain; that we had abandoned that Union for which we have so often periled our lives."

How did the "bayonet vote" help Lincoln win reelection in 1864?

Shortly before election day, many Northern soldiers were furloughed home so that they could vote, presumably for Lincoln. Other soldiers were permitted to vote at the front. This so-called "bayonet vote" added to Lincoln's winning margin over McClellan. (See page 169 for the 1864 election results.)

What Democrat wept bitterly when he was nominated for the presidency in 1868?

Horatio Seymour, the permanent chairman of the convention and a former governor of New York. Seymour was not a candidate for the presidency, but the convention became hopelessly deadlocked, and on the 22nd ballot the Ohio delegation switched its votes to him. Greatly agitated, Seymour came to the rostrum and said, "Gentlemen, I thank you, and may God bless you for your kindness to me, but your candidate I cannot be."

The head of the Ohio delegation refused to withdraw Seymour's name, so the New Yorker headed to the rostrum to decline again. But midway across the platform Seymour was stopped by some of the Democratic leaders, picked up from the floor, whisked out of the hall, and taken to a nearby club. While Seymour was absent, a stampede for him developed, and he was nominated for the presidency by a unanimous vote.

When he learned of the convention's decision, Seymour wept and hesitated, but finally accepted the nomination.

What Civil War hero did the Republicans run for the presidency in 1868?

General Ulysses S. Grant.

What new group of voters helped Grant win a majority of the popular vote?

The newly enfranchised blacks. They cast about 500,000 ballots for Grant, who won the election by only a little more than 300,000 votes. If the election had been restricted to white voters, Democrat Seymour would have won more popular votes but probably not more electoral votes than Grant. This election demonstrated how the new but important black vote helped the Republicans and hurt the Democrats in the period following the Civil War. (See page 170 for the 1868 election results.)

How did it happen that Horace Greeley was the presidential nominee of both the Liberal Republicans and the Democrats in 1872?

Grant's first term in the White House was tainted by widespread corruption and criticized for the "carpetbag" governments it sponsored in the South. Reformers within the Republican Party broke with the regulars and formed the Liberal Republican Party. They nominated Horace Greeley, editor of the *New York Tribune*, to run for the presidency.

Two months later the Democratic convention met and, not wanting to divide the anti-Grant vote, also nominated Greeley as their presidential candidate. This was ironic, since Greeley, as a newspaper editor, often had severely criticized Democratic officeholders.

But even though Greeley carried the banners of two parties, President Grant was easily reelected. (See page 169 for the 1872 election results.)

Why didn't Greeley win a single electoral vote in the 1872 election?

Horace Greeley was the only presidential nominee who died between election day and the time when the presidential electors cast their official ballots. The 66 Democratic electors who would have voted for Greeley divided their votes among various prominent Democrats.

Near the end of his life, Greeley's misfortunes were almost incredible. Within a single month in 1872 he lost his wife, his election for the presidency, his newspaper job, his sanity and his life.

What two governors were the Democratic and Republican nominees in the famous disputed election of 1876?

Democratic Governor Samuel J. Tilden of New York and Republican Governor Rutherford B. Hayes of Ohio. Tilden won the popular vote and led in the electoral vote, but Congress appointed a special electoral commission to decide who had won the electoral votes of the states in which the returns were disputed. The electoral commission awarded the election to Hayes. (See pages 163-165 for more information about this contested election and the 1876 election results.)

Whom did the Democrats nominate to head their ticket in the 1880 election?

Ulysses S. Grant had been elected to the White House for two terms chiefly because of his popularity as a Civil War general, so in 1880 the Democrats nominated for the presidency General Winfield Hancock of Pennsylvania, an officer on the Union side in the Battle of Gettysburg. General Hancock (who weighed 250 pounds) was friendly and well liked but colorless as a political candidate. The *Chicago Tribune* dismissed Hancock as a nonentity who "does nothing but eat, drink, and enjoy himself sensually."

In 1880 the Republicans set their party record for the most ballots cast before a presidential nominee was selected. What dark horse candidate finally won the nomination?

Congressman James A. Garfield of Ohio, who won the Republican nomination on the 36th ballot and the election in November. (See pages 162 and 163 for the 1880 election results.)

The nickname for the Republican Party was widely used for the first time at the 1880 convention. What is it?

GOP, which stands for "Grand Old Party." The origin of this nickname is unknown, but about the time that it became popular Great Britain's Prime Minister William Gladstone was fondly called the Grand Old Man, and perhaps some Republican admirers of Gladstone may have applied the same term of affection to their political party. It is ironic, however, that the GOP is more than a half century younger than the Democratic Party!

About what Democratic nominee was it said that his friends "love him most for the enemies he has made"?

Congressman Edward Bragg of Wisconsin made this now-famous remark about New York Governor Grover Cleveland, who won the 1884 presidential nomination despite strong opposition from the corruption-riddled Tammany Hall political machine in his own home state. Two Tammany Hall delegates played a dirty trick on Cleveland when they asked to give seconding speeches for his nomination and then used the opportunity to condemn the man whose candidacy they supposedly were endorsing.

How did it happen that the chief issue in the 1884 presidential campaign was public dishonesty versus private immorality?

The Republican presidential nominee in 1884, James G. Blaine of Maine, had served as Speaker of the House, as a senator, and as Secretary of State. But the Maine politician's public reputation was tarnished because he allegedly had used his strong influence in Congress to help a railroad company and received in return the right to sell the company's bonds and pocket a very high commission. A famous political cartoon showed Blaine, clad only in underpants, as the "tattooed man," whose body was covered with ugly terms related to his shady financial deals.

Blaine's Democratic opponent, Grover Cleveland, had acquired a reputation for great integrity and complete honesty as mayor of Buffalo and later governor of New York. His enemies, however, discovered that in his youth Cleveland had had an illicit affair with a Buffalo woman and could have fathered her illegitimate child. Even though the woman had several suitors, any one of whom might have been the child's father, Cleveland was the only one who admitted any responsibility for the pregnancy, and he made payments to help support the child.

When the Republicans uncovered this story about Cleveland's past, they invented this chant: "Ma! Ma! Where's my Pa?" To which the Democrats replied: "Gone to the White House. Ha! Ha! Ha!"

The election was hard fought, and Cleveland barely defeated Blaine. (See page 154 for the 1884 election results.)

Whom did President Cleveland run against when he sought reelection in 1888?

Former Senator Benjamin Harrison of Indiana, who won the 1884 Republican presidential nomination on the eighth ballot.

Harrison trailed in the popular vote but won a majority of the
electoral vote and drove Cleveland out of the White House. (See
pages 165 and 166 for the 1888 election results.)

Four years later, did former President Cleveland have difficulty winning his party's nomination to run against President Harrison in the 1892 election?

No. In spite of opposition again from Tammany Hall, Cleveland was nominated on the first ballot. For the first time both
the Democrats and the Republicans pitted Presidents against
each other, and Cleveland emerged the winner. His victory was
due, in part, to many Republicans voting for James B. Weaver,
the Populist Party candidate. Weaver amassed more than one
million votes, most of which probably would have gone to
Harrison if the Populist nominee had not entered the contest.
(See pages 154 and 155 for the 1892 election results.)

Who was Vice-President during Cleveland's second term in the White House?

Adlai E. Stevenson of Illinois, who had been a congressman
and was first assistant United States Postmaster General in
Cleveland's first term. He was the grandfather of the 1952 and
1956 Democratic presidential nominee.

What was the chief issue that divided Democrats at their convention in 1896?

The chief issue was the currency question. Eastern delegates
generally supported a hard-money policy and the continuation
of the gold standard. Most Southern and Western delegates
called for a soft-money policy with the unlimited coinage of
silver at a ratio of 16 ounces of silver to every ounce of gold.

How did this one issue set the stage for the most famous speech ever delivered at a political convention?

During the platform debate on currency, the closing speaker
on the silver side was William Jennings Bryan, a former congressman from Nebraska. Bryan used this occasion to deliver his
famous "Cross of Gold" speech, which concluded with the
memorable sentence "You shall not press down upon the brow
of labor this crown of thorns, you shall not crucify mankind
upon a cross of gold." Bryan's magnificent voice reached every

part of the great hall, and he later wrote that the spellbound audience responded "like a trained choir."

Actually, Bryan's speech was not extemporaneous. He had tried out parts of it on various Midwestern audiences, and whenever the crowds loudly applauded a point that he made, Bryan remembered the remark and included it in his "Cross of Gold" speech.

Did the "Cross of Gold" speech affect the selection of the Democratic presidential nominee in 1896?

Yes. Before the convention assembled, Senator Richard P. Bland of Missouri was favored to win the nomination, and the 36-year-old Bryan was not considered a major candidate. In fact, the Bryan delegation from Nebraska was not even seated until after it won a credentials fight against a gold-standard delegation from the same state. Bland led Bryan by a 235-to-137-vote margin on the first ballot, but Bryan overtook the Missouri senator on the fourth ballot and won the nomination on the fifth ballot. Undoubtedly, his spine-tingling address was a major factor in converting delegates to his candidacy.

What type of campaign did the candidates wage in 1896?

William Jennings Bryan conducted a barnstorming campaign that took him from Nebraska to Maine and from the Southern states to the Canadian border. All together, he said, he covered over 18,000 miles, made about 600 speeches, and addressed possibly five million people. To prevent the loss of his voice, Bryan used all sorts of cough drops, gargles, and throat compresses. But his powerful voice held out to the end of the arduous campaign, which was much more active and strenuous than that waged by any other candidate in the nineteenth century.

By contrast, the Republican candidate, Governor William McKinley of Ohio, stayed at his home in Canton during the campaign. From his front porch he spoke to hundreds of delegations that had been transported to his hometown by railroads at cut-rate prices.

Despite his extensive speech making and the fact that in 1896 he was the nominee of both the Democrats and the Populists, Bryan lost the election to McKinley. (See pages 171 and 172 for the 1896 election results.)

When Bryan ran again for the presidency in 1900, was free silver still the chief issue?

No. The discovery of huge new gold deposits in Alaska and the subsequent increase in currency had led to the decline of the controversial free silver issue. Bryan, however, threatened to disavow his presidential candidacy if the convention refused to include a plank in its platform calling once again for the unlimited coinage of silver. So the delegates dutifully, but somewhat reluctantly, voted to insert a prosilver plank in the party platform.

The Democrats' major issue in 1900 was imperialism. Two years earlier the United States had liberated Spanish colonies as a result of the Spanish-American War, and the Democrats were highly critical of President McKinley's policies toward the Philippine Islands, Puerto Rico, and Cuba. The Democratic platform proclaimed "that no nation can long endure half republic and half empire." Bryan was especially incensed by the government's decision to keep the Philippines as an American colony. He strongly asserted that the United States should set up a stable government in the Philippines and then give the Filipinos independence.

The American public, however, was not deeply concerned about imperialism. Prosperity reigned, and President McKinley was easily reelected. (See page 172 for the 1900 election results.)

In 1904 the Democrats deserted liberal, colorful Bryan for a conservative, colorless candidate. Who was he?

Judge Alton B. Parker of the New York Court of Appeals. When Parker won the nomination and learned that the currency issue was not included in the party platform, he astounded the convention by sending a telegram declaring his support for the gold standard and offering to decline the nomination if this was unsatisfactory to the majority of delegates. Bryan was infuriated by Parker's stand, but the convention responded that the currency question had been omitted from the platform because it was no longer an issue, and Parker's approval of the gold standard was acceptable.

What prominent newspaper publisher sought the Democratic presidential nomination in 1904 and finished second to Parker

in the balloting?

William Randolph Hearst, who won 200 votes on the first ballot.

What was unusual about the Democratic vice-presidential nominee in 1904?

He was former West Virginia Senator Henry G. Davis, who at age 80 was the oldest nominee ever to run on a national ticket selected by either major party.

What Republican candidate won the 1904 election by a record-breaking margin in the popular vote?

The popular Theodore Roosevelt, who had been elevated to the presidency after the assassination of William McKinley in 1901. (See pages 168 and 169 for the 1904 election results.)

After he had been defeated for the presidency in 1896 and 1900, did William Jennings Bryan ever get another chance to run for the nation's highest office?

Yes. Having lost badly with Parker and conservatism in the 1904 campaign, the Democrats were ready for Bryan again, and in 1908 they nominated him on the first ballot. The Republican candidate was President Theodore Roosevelt's hand-picked successor, Secretary of War William Howard Taft. Bryan could not overcome the Republican tide, and his defeat by Taft gave him the unenviable distinction of being the only Democrat who was a three-time loser for the presidency.

What happened within the Republican Party in 1912 that improved the Democrats' chances of capturing the presidency for the first time since Cleveland left the White House in 1897?

A serious rift developed between former President Theodore Roosevelt and his successor, President William Howard Taft. Both men sought the 1912 Republican nomination, and when Taft, who controlled the party machinery, was victorious, Roosevelt bolted the GOP and became the presidential candidate of the Progressive Party. Some Republicans, mainly conservatives, stayed loyal to Taft, but a large faction of the GOP supported the reform-minded Roosevelt. With the Republicans badly divided, the Democrats had an ideal opportunity to win back the White House.

With a possible victory looming on the political horizon, were the Democrats united at their 1912 convention?

No. First, there was a savage battle when Bryan opposed the national committee's choice of Alton B. Parker for temporary chairman. The convention voted to seat Parker by 579 votes to 508, but this triggered a flood of about 100,000 telegrams condemning the delegates for repudiating Bryan.

Later, six candidates vied for the presidential nomination, each intent on becoming his party's standard-bearer in a year when the Democrats had a superb chance to regain the White House. In the preconvention struggle Speaker of the House James B. "Champ" Clark of Missouri had lined up the most delegates and was favored to win the nomination.

How did Bryan help prevent the Democrats from nominating Clark?

On the tenth roll call New York shifted its 90 votes from Ohio Governor Judson Harmon to Clark, giving the House Speaker 556 votes, which was a majority of the delegate votes. Although Clark needed 730 votes to win the necessary two-thirds majority, no Democratic presidential candidate since 1844 had won a simple majority of votes and failed to gain the nomination. So Clark's followers, anticipating victory, staged a frenzied hour-long demonstration for their candidate.

The celebration for Clark, however, was premature. On the 14th ballot Bryan surprised the convention by announcing that he would no longer vote for Clark, since he now had New York's support and might fall under the sinister influence of Tammany Hall. Instead, Bryan declared, he was switching his vote to Governor Woodrow Wilson of New Jersey, who was Clark's closest rival in the balloting.

It is uncertain whether Bryan genuinely supported Wilson or simply hoped that a deadlocked convention might turn to him as a compromise candidate. In either case, Bryan effectively halted the bandwagon for Clark, whose vote total never again reached its previous height.

After Clark's lead declined, did Wilson easily win the Democratic nomination?

No. Wilson wasn't nominated until the 46th roll call, which

was the largest number of ballots cast by a Democratic convention since 1860, when the North-South division at the Charleston convention failed to provide a nominee after 57 ballots.

In the general election the governor of New Jersey defeated two presidents, Taft and Roosevelt. (See page 151 for the 1912 election results.)

Wilson was elected President on a platform calling for major reforms. Which of these reforms were achieved during his administration?

The Democratic platform in 1912 called for tariff reduction, more effective antitrust measures, improvements in the banking system, and the ratification of Constitutional amendments calling for an income tax and the direct election of United States senators. All of these major reforms—and some other ones— were achieved during Wilson's time in the White House.

When Wilson ran for a second term in 1916, did he win reelection easily?

No. The Republicans were reunited in 1916, and their candidate, Supreme Court Justice Charles Evans Hughes, gave the incumbent President a very tough battle. Wilson's victory was by the narrowest electoral-vote margin of any presidential election to date in the twentieth century. (See pages 155 and 156 for more information about this fascinating campaign and the 1916 election results.)

CAMPAIGN TRAILS,
1920-1976

Dark horse candidates were nominated for the presidency by both the Democrats and the Republicans in 1920. Who were these candidates?

The Democrats selected Governor James M. Cox of Ohio, who finished third on the first roll call and didn't win the nomination until the 44th ballot. The Republicans chose Senator Warren G. Harding of Ohio, who was in sixth place after the first roll call and won the nomination on the 10th ballot.

Two future Presidents were nominated for the vice-presidency in 1920. Who were they?

The Democrats nominated Assistant Secretary of the Navy Franklin D. Roosevelt. (This was one year before he was stricken with polio.) The Republicans nominated Governor Calvin Coolidge of Massachusetts.

What was the most controversial and emotional issue in the 1920 election?

The Senate's rejection of the Treaty of Versailles, which created the League of Nations. Cox strongly supported the League, and the Democratic Party in the first plank in its platform said that it "favors the League of Nations as the surest, if not the only, practicable means of maintaining the permanent peace of the world and terminating the insufferable burden of great military and naval establishments."

The Republican Party platform praised the Senate for rejecting the League but called for a vague "agreement among the nations to preserve the peace of the world." Harding straddled the League issue during the campaign and stressed instead America's desire to "return to normalcy."

The Republican message appealed to a majority of voters, and the ticket of Harding and Coolidge trounced Cox and Roosevelt. This was the only election FDR ever lost. (See page 168 for the 1920 election results.)

What two wings of the Democratic Party engaged in a long, bitter struggle to gain control of the 1924 convention?

The urban and rural wings battled to dominate the Democratic convention. Urban delegates generally favored the nomination of Governor Alfred E. Smith of New York, a Catholic from a poor family of Irish immigrants who lived in the tenements of New York City. Smith opposed Prohibition and the Ku Klux Klan. The rural delegates' candidate was William G. McAdoo of California, who championed Prohibition and was tolerant of the Ku Klux Klan.

The two factions were almost evenly divided. This was demonstrated by the convention vote on a controversial amendment to denounce the Ku Klux Klan by name. Most urban delegates supported the plank; most rural delegates opposed it. The plank was defeated by the extremely close margin of 543.15 to 542.35 votes.

What all-time record was set by the 1924 Democratic convention?

Neither of the two factions—urban and rural—would support the other's candidate, so the convention took nine days of balloting and 103 roll calls before it selected a presidential nominee. The compromise candidate who was finally nominated was John W. Davis of West Virginia, a conservative lawyer who practiced in New York City.

The Democrats named the brother of a famous politician as their vice-presidential candidate in 1924. Who was he?

Governor Charles W. Bryan of Nebraska, the younger brother of William Jennings Bryan. However, the younger Bryan had no more luck than his brother had in winning a national election. The Republican ticket of Calvin Coolidge (who had been elevated to the presidency after the death of Harding in 1923) and

Charles G. Dawes easily defeated Davis and Bryan. (See page 170 for the 1924 election results.)

Did the Democrats have another prolonged battle at their 1928 convention?

No. In 1928 the Democrats were determined to achieve unity and avoid the kind of donnybrook that had torn their party apart four years before. For the third time Franklin D. Roosevelt made the nominating speech for his friend and fellow New Yorker, Alfred E. Smith, and this time the Democrats selected Smith as their standard-bearer on the first ballot.

Why was Al Smith one of the most colorful campaigners in our political history?

Smith had a captivating personality, a sharp wit, and an ability to spice his extemporaneous speeches with pungent expressions. His familiar hallmarks were a brown derby hat, a lively campaign song ("The Sidewalks of New York") and a penchant for pronouncing "radio" as "raddio."

Why did Republican Herbert Hoover defeat Smith in the 1928 election?

Smith's Catholicism lost him many votes, expecially in the traditionally Democratic rural South. Ridiculous stories abounded that if Smith were elected, the Pope would move into the White House and Catholics would take over the country. Also, Smith's belief that Prohibition was not effective cost him support throughout the Protestant "Bible Belt."

Nevertheless, Smith would have lost the election to Hoover even if he had been a Protestant and had supported Prohibition. Times were prosperous, and the public was in no mood to desert the Republican Party, which had reigned during the dazzling twenties. Ironically, it was probably fortunate for the Democrats that Smith was beaten, for if he had won, he instead of Hoover would have been the scapegoat for the Great Depression that descended on the country in 1929. (See page 168 for the 1928 election results.)

Franklin D. Roosevelt won his first presidential nomination in 1932. Was it an easy victory?

No. New York Governor Roosevelt had two strong rivals for the Democratic nomination—his former friend now turned foe,

Alfred E. Smith of New York, and House Speaker John Nance Garner of Texas. On the first roll call FDR led the balloting, but he was more than 100 votes shy of the necessary two-thirds majority. He picked up only a few votes on the second and third ballots, and his managers grew concerned that the convention might become deadlocked and turn to a compromise candidate. But Garner wanted to avoid a drawn-out battle at any cost, and on the fourth ballot the California delegation switched its 44 votes from him to FDR. This set in motion a bandwagon that carried Roosevelt to the nomination before a fifth roll call could be taken.

It is not known whether a deal was made with Garner, but the House Speaker was the unanimous choice of the convention for the vice-presidency.

What tradition did FDR break at the 1932 convention?

He flew to the Chicago convention to accept its presidential nomination in person. Addressing the convention, he declared he had broken the tradition that the "candidate should remain in professed ignorance of what has happened for weeks until he is formally notified of that event many weeks later . . . . You have nominated me and I know it, and I am here to thank you for the honor."

How did the term "New Deal" originate?

In his acceptance speech at the 1932 convention, Roosevelt concluded, "I pledge you, I pledge myself to a new deal for the American people." The next day a cartoonist took from FDR's speech the words "new deal"—a term to which Roosevelt had attached no special significance—and used it in a political cartoon. Henceforth, "New Deal" became the hallmark of the Roosevelt program.

How did political correspondent Walter Lippmann describe FDR in 1932?

Lippmann said Roosevelt was "a pleasant man who, without any important qualifications for the office, would very much like to be President."

"I accuse the present administration of being the greatest spending administration in peace times in all our history. It is an

administration that has piled bureau on bureau, commission on commission." Did Hoover make this statement about FDR's administration?

No. Roosevelt made this statement about Hoover's administration during the 1932 election campaign. FDR also promised that if he were elected President, he would slash government spending by 25 percent.

Regardless of how the voters felt about Roosevelt's promises, they elected him in 1932 to his first term in the White House. (See page 150 for the 1932 election results.)

An audience of 100,000—breaking all records for the size of a political meeting—heard Roosevelt say, "This generation of Americans has a rendezvous with destiny." When did this happen?

It happened in June 1936 at Franklin Field in Philadelphia, when Roosevelt accepted the Democratic nomination for his reelection. The 1936 convention had finally abandoned the rule that the winning candidate needed a two-thirds majority of the delegates' votes, but, ironically, this was the first Democratic convention since 1840 when there was no need for a single roll call, because FDR and Garner were renominated by acclamation.

The election in 1936 was a referendum on the New Deal, and Roosevelt won a huge victory over his Republican opponent, Governor Alfred M. Landon of Kansas. (See page 150 for the 1936 election results.)

When did a "no" from FDR mean "yes" to a Democratic convention?

For several months before the 1940 convention a "Draft Roosevelt" movement was gaining converts among Democrats, but the President remained silent about his intentions to run for a third term. Shortly after the convention opened, Senator Alben Barkley of Kentucky declared that he had a message from the President. This was a tense moment, for some delegates thought FDR might shut the door on the movement to draft him. But the statement from the White House merely indicated that the President did not desire to run for reelection and that "all the delegates are free to vote for any candidate."

FDR had said "no" in such a mild way that the delegates interpreted it as a "yes" to the draft movement, and Barkley's message from the White House was greeted with a jubilant

45-minute demonstration for the President who said he didn't
want to run again.

Two of Roosevelt's closest associates vied with him for the 1940 presidential nomination. Who were they?

Vice-President John Nance Garner and Postmaster General
James A. Farley, who was also the national chairman of the
Democratic Party and FDR's political manager in his previous
races for the White House. But neither Garner nor Farley had a
strong following, and Roosevelt won renomination on the
first ballot.

After FDR had been renominated in 1940, why did he threaten the convention that he might not accept the nomination?

Roosevelt informed the convention that since Vice-President
Garner would not run again with him, he wanted Agriculture
Secretary Henry A. Wallace of Iowa as his new running mate.
Wallace was too liberal for many conservative Democrats, but
FDR gave the convention an ultimatum to accept his hand-
picked nominee or he would not head the ticket. Roosevelt got
his way, but Wallace was such an unpopular choice that he was
not even allowed to address the delegates.

In 1940 the Republican convention nominated a presidential candidate who had been a Democrat until two years before. Who was he?

Wendell L. Willkie of Indiana, who had never before run for
political office.

What was the most emotional issue in the 1940 election?

The question of whether Roosevelt should have a third term
as President and thus defy the two-term tradition started by
George Washington. Willkie solemnly proclaimed that if FDR
was elected for a third term, "our democratic system will not
outlast another four years." (Actually, Roosevelt was not the
first President to seek a third term; Ulysses S. Grant in 1880
and Theodore Roosevelt in 1912 both had tried unsuccessfully
to accomplish the same feat.)

The voters decided to set aside the two-term tradition and
reelected FDR by a large margin. (See page 150 for the 1940
election results.)

Did Roosevelt keep the 1944 convention in suspense about whether he would run for a fourth term?

No. In 1944 the United States was at war—for the first time during a presidential election year since 1864. FDR, who had been coy about his intentions four years before, announced a week before the 1944 convention opened that he would accept renomination like a "good soldier."

How did Roosevelt manipulate the selection of his running mate in 1944?

First, Roosevelt wrote a letter to the chairman of the convention stating that if he were a delegate he would vote for the renomination of Vice-President Wallace but that the convention could do as it wished. This lukewarm endorsement, which was read to the delegates, was the kiss of death for Wallace, who obviously lacked the President's wholehearted support. Later a letter was made public that FDR had written to Democratic Party National Chairman Robert E. Hannegan, saying he would be pleased to run with either Missouri Senator Harry Truman or Supreme Court Justice William O. Douglas. Finally, Roosevelt phoned Truman at the convention and prevailed on him to accept the nomination.

The Roosevelt-Truman ticket defeated the Republican ticket of Governor Thomas E. Dewey of New York and Ohio Governor John W. Bricker. So FDR started his fourth term in the White House, but it ended less than three months later when he died on April 12, 1945. (See page 150 for the 1944 election results.)

With Roosevelt dead and President Truman under heavy attack, did the Democrats seek anyone outside their party to run for the presidency in 1948?

Yes. Many Democrats concluded that President Truman was too unpopular to be returned to the White House in 1948, and they began hunting for a substitute candidate. Several months before the convention some prominent party leaders, including James Roosevelt, FDR's eldest son, approached General Dwight D. Eisenhower to see if the World War II hero would be their presidential nominee. The general turned down the offer and refused to say whether he was a Democrat or a Republican. Some Democrats then turned to liberal Supreme Court Justice William O. Douglas, but when he also refused to become a candidate, the effort to find a replacement for Truman evaporated.

Who championed a strong civil rights plank for the 1948 Democratic Party platform, which caused some of the Southern delegates to walk out of the convention?

Hubert H. Humphrey, the young mayor of Minneapolis and a candidate for the United States Senate. After the civil rights plank was adopted, the entire Mississippi delegation and half of the Alabama delegation walked out of the convention.

Did most of the Southern delegates at the 1948 convention vote for Truman's renomination, despite his strong support for civil rights?

No. More than 90 percent of the remaining Southern delegates cast their ballots for Georgia Senator Richard B. Russell, whose total vote count on the first ballot was 266. But this did not jeopardize the renomination of President Truman, who won 926 votes on the first and only roll call. Additional delegates switched their votes to Truman when it became apparent that he was the winner, swelling his total of 947½.

The Democrats nominated their keynote speaker at the 1948 convention as Truman's running mate. Who was he?

Senator Alben W. Barkley of Kentucky. Although President Truman preferred William O. Douglas as the vice-presidential candidate, when the Supreme Court justice refused to permit his name to be offered, the convention turned to the 70-year-old Barkley, whose spellbinding keynote address had produced a spontaneous demonstration that lasted for half an hour.

How did President Truman enliven the 1948 convention when he appeared there to make his acceptance speech?

President Truman flew from Washington to Philadelphia and addressed the dispirited, bleary-eyed delegates shortly before 2:00 A.M. He delivered a fiery speech that castigated the Republican 80th Congress as the worst Congress, and he called the lawmakers back into special session to give the Republicans another chance to pass badly needed legislation.

Truman's fighting speech brought the tired delegates to their feet, cheering and clapping, and the spunky little man from Missouri kept fighting throughout his uphill campaign. On election day he defeated the heavily favored Republican nominee, New York Governor Thomas E. Dewey, and two other former

Democrats who were heading third-party tickets. (See pages 156-158 for more information about this exciting campaign and the 1948 election results.)

When President Truman retired from the White House, there was a wide-open race for the Democratic presidential nomination in 1952. Who was the early front-runner?

Senator Estes Kefauver of Tennessee, who had gained national attention by chairing a Senate crime investigation committee that held spectacular televised sessions. Kefauver won 12 of the 15 state primary elections, ranging from the first one in New Hampshire to the last one in California, and nearly two-thirds of all the Democrats who voted in the primaries cast their ballots for him.

What was Kefauver's emblem in the 1952 campaign?

A coonskin cap. Short on money and organization, Kefauver waged a vigorous hand-shaking campaign on Main Streets throughout the country, and sometimes the lanky Tennessean donned a coonskin cap to enhance the homespun, Lincolnesque image that he was trying to convey to the voters.

Since Kefauver was so popular with the rank-and-file voters, why didn't he win the presidential nomination?

His popularity did not spill over to the Southern conservatives, who found him too liberal, to the party leaders, who felt he was shallow and not a good team player, or to the big-city bosses, who were embarrassed because his televised exposé on crime had often pointed the finger of guilt at local politicians doing business with gangsters.

The 1952 Democratic nominee was the most reluctant candidate to run for the presidency since Horatio Seymour in 1868. Who was he?

Governor Adlai E. Stevenson of Illinois, who insisted that his only ambition was to run for a second term in the Illinois statehouse. He did not campaign in any of the state primaries, and he vehemently rebuked any and all offers of support from those who wanted him to head the presidential ticket. But the Illinois governor was the first choice of many party chieftains, and even he was powerless to resist a "Draft Stevenson" movement that had gained tremendous momentum by the time the 1952 convention opened.

Eleven names were placed in nomination, and Senator Kefauver led on the first two ballots. The party leaders, however, prevailed. On the third ballot the reluctant Stevenson emerged as the Democratic standard-bearer.

What was unusual about Stevenson's marital status?

He was the first presidential nominee of either major party who had been divorced.

Since Stevenson had not sought the 1952 nomination, did he wage a reticent campaign?

No. Stevenson waged a hard-hitting campaign, and he impressed both friends and foes with his exceptional eloquence. Seldom if ever in our history has the public been treated to political speeches that matched Stevenson's for intellectual content, urbane wit, graceful phrasing, and dynamic delivery. At the time of the 1952 convention the Illinois governor was scarcely known to people outside his state. By the end of the campaign, thanks to his televised speeches, this balding, slight, rather homely man was admired and respected by many millions of Americans from Maine to Oregon.

Nevertheless, in the election Stevenson was pitted against a living legend, General Dwight D. Eisenhower, and the greatly beloved Ike won an easy victory. (See page 168 for the 1952 results.)

Four years later, in 1956, did Kefauver enter and win most of the primaries, while Stevenson again sat on the sidelines?

No. Kefauver won primaries in nine (mainly small) states, but Stevenson was the victor in the primaries of such heavily populated states as Pennsylvania, California, and Illinois. Kefauver dropped out of the race before the convention met and threw his support to Stevenson.

Whom did former President Truman support at the 1956 Democratic convention?

Labeling Adlai Stevenson a "defeatist," the ex-President endorsed the candidacy of liberal New York Governor Averell Harriman. Truman appeared at the convention and seconded the nomination of Harriman.

What famous woman told the convention she wanted to see Stevenson given a second chance to win the presidency?

Eleanor Roosevelt. Most of the delegates agreed with Mrs. Roosevelt, and Stevenson was nominated on the first ballot.

After his nomination but before his acceptance speech, Stevenson made a surprise appearance before the convention. Why did he do this?

To announce that he was leaving the choice of a running mate to the delegates. This astonishing statement nearly threw a cut-and-dried convention into bedlam and sent a host of ambitious politicians scurrying to line up votes as they frantically sought the vice-presidential nomination.

Who were the chief contenders for the second spot on the Democratic ticket?

There were 13 candidates, but the major ones were Tennessee Senators Estes Kefauver and Albert Gore, Senator John F. Kennedy of Massachusetts, Senator Hubert H. Humphrey of Minnesota, and Mayor Robert F. Wagner of New York.

On the first ballot Kefauver had 483½ votes, Kennedy 304, Gore 178, Wagner 162½, and Humphrey 134½.

Who spurted into the lead on the second ballot?

Kennedy moved into the lead, and the young senator was only 39 votes short of the nomination after Kentucky switched its 30 votes to him following the second ballot.

What happened to prevent Kennedy from capturing the vice-presidential nomination?

Just when it appeared that Kennedy was going over the top, Gore suddenly withdrew from the race in favor of Kefauver, and Humphrey followed suit. Other state delegations quickly switched their votes, and Kefauver, who had seemed certain of defeat only a short time before, emerged as the surprise winner and Stevenson's running mate.

Intellectual, fluent Stevenson and plain-speaking Kefauver with his coonskin cap were a dissimilar pair, and they appealed to different intellectual strata of American society. But neither could match the voter appeal of President Eisenhower, who easily won a second term in the White House. (See page 168 for the 1956 election results.)

How did Kennedy's loss at the 1956 convention affect his political future?

It was an enormous blessing in disguise. If Kennedy had been Stevenson's running mate, he would have been part of the ticket that was crushed by the Eisenhower landslide.

Often it has been said that the determined young senator from Massachusetts began to run for the presidency in 1960 the day after the 1956 election. This would have been a much more difficult, perhaps impossible mission if Kennedy had been forced to construct his campaign from the ashes of defeat.

What obstacles did Kennedy have to overcome when he entered the 1960 presidential campaign?

The most serious obstacle was his Catholic religion. Many voters had rejected Al Smith because of his religion in 1928, and there was still strong resistance to sending a Catholic to the White House. Kennedy's age (he was 42 when the campaign began) was also a problem because some people considered him too young and immature for the awesome responsibilities that a President must shoulder. His extreme wealth was another handicap, and the charge that the Kennedys wanted to buy the White House was often repeated. Moreover, the Massachusetts senator had compiled only a mediocre record in Congress, and he had frequently been absent when key votes were taken.

Why did Kennedy enter most of the state primaries?

Because he faced so many obstacles, Kennedy felt that he had to put his candidacy before the voters and prove in the state primaries that he was a winner.

Kennedy carried the first primary in New Hampshire, but he had no organized opposition in that state. Next came Wisconsin, where Kennedy competed against Senator Hubert H. Humphrey of Minnesota. The results were clouded, with Kennedy gaining six of the state's ten districts, but Humphrey made a good showing in this state, which neighbors Minnesota. The first real test of Kennedy's strength was in West Viriginia, where anti-Catholicism was a formidable factor. Kennedy and Humphrey both campaigned vigorously for the convention delegates from this small state, but the large funds that the Massachusetts millionaire spent on building a strong organization and television ads paid rich dividends. Kennedy swept to victory in West Virginia, and Humphrey then dropped out of the race. In other state primaries Kennedy carried Illinois, Massachusetts, Pennsylvania, Indiana, Nebraska, Maryland, and Oregon.

Who was Kennedy's chief rival when the 1960 Democratic convention assembled in Los Angeles?

Senate Majority Leader Lyndon B. Johnson, who had strong support from Southern delegations. Johnson challenged Kennedy to a debate before the joint Texas and Massachusetts delegations, but it was held the day before balloting began, when most delegates had already made up their minds.

In 1960 was there any attempt to launch another "Draft Stevenson" movement?

Yes. The former Illinois governor had been uncertain about whether to toss his hat into the ring for a third try at the presidency. But after his name was offered for nomination, Stevenson's supporters staged a wild, passionate demonstration for the elder statesman of their party, which was greeted by uproarious cheering from the galleries. (It was later discovered that most of the paraders in the aisles were not delegates, and the galleries had been packed with Stevenson fans, most of whom had acquired their tickets by questionable means.)

The effort to start a bandwagon in Stevenson's direction failed. Kennedy won the nomination on the first ballot with 806 votes to 409 for Johnson and only 79½ for Stevenson.

What was the biggest surprise at the 1960 convention?

Kennedy asked Johnson to be his running mate, and the Senate majority leader accepted the offer. Politicians were stunned by Johnson's decision, since they felt he was stepping down from a position of great power in the Senate to run for an office that carried much less clout.

But this turned out to be a stroke of genius for the Democrats. Southerner Johnson played a major role in helping Northerner Kennedy carry the states of Texas, North and South Carolina, Louisiana, and Arkansas. Without most of these states, the Democratic ticket would have lost the close election.

By what dramatic event did Kennedy partly dispel the issue of his religion?

Kennedy faced the religious issue squarely when he addressed the Greater Houston Ministerial Association, which was composed mainly of Protestant preachers in the "Bible Belt." The Catholic candidate stated that he strongly believed in the separation of church and state and, if elected President, he would formulate all policies "without regard to religious pressures or dictates." Kennedy's televised speech was so convincing that taped copies of it were shown later in the campaign at various other locations within the "Bible Belt."

How did an incident involving Martin Luther King, Jr., boost Kennedy's support among blacks?

King had been jailed for taking part in a civil rights "sit-in" attempt in an Atlanta restaurant. Kennedy phoned King's wife to offer his support, and the next day he helped arrange the black leader's release on bail.

What was the most unusual feature of the 1960 presidential campaign?

This was the first time in our history that the presidential nominees of the two major parties engaged in a series of televised debates that were beamed to the nation. There were four hour-long debates between Kennedy and his Republican opponent, Vice-President Richard Nixon. The first debate was watched by 70 to 75 million people, and the other three drew audiences between 61 and 65 million.

In polls taken after the first debate, television viewers gave Kennedy a slight edge, while radio listeners favored Nixon's performance. This interesting discrepancy may have occurred because the TV audience noticed some things that would not have been known by those who heard the debate on the radio— Kennedy appeared more confident, poised and aggressive, while Nixon looked tired and ill at ease, and his appearance suffered from the stubble of a beard that could be observed in the glare of bright television lights.

More than anything else, the debates gave Kennedy the opportunity to display his tremendous charisma to nationwide audiences and to assure the voters that he was not too young or immature to be President.

Nixon was the first presidential nominee to campaign in all 50 states. Was this a good idea?

It probably was not a good idea because while Nixon was crisscrossing the country and spending much time in the smaller states, Kennedy was concentrating most of his time and attention on the heavily populated states that had large blocs of electoral votes. In the election Kennedy won only 23 states, but he had most of the large states in his victory column. (See pages 153 and 154 for the 1960 election results.)

Besides running for the vice-presidency, what other office did Johnson run for in November 1960?

He ran for reelection to the Senate from Texas. Johnson won both elections! On January 3, 1961, he was sworn in as senator for a third term; he resigned three minutes later. On January 20, 1961, he was inaugurated as Vice-President.

Before Kennedy's election, how long had it been since a United States senator was elected President?

Forty years had passed since Republican Senator Warren G. Harding of Ohio had been elected to the presidency in 1920. Also like Kennedy, President Harding died in office before completing the third year of his first term.

Did President Lyndon B. Johnson face any competition at the 1964 Democratic convention when he sought to run for a full four-year term?

No. Without holding a roll call vote, the convention nominated Johnson by acclamation.

After his nomination, how did Johnson surprise the convention?

He took the unprecedented step of appearing before the convention to announce his choice for the vice-presidency, Senator Hubert H. Humphrey of Minnesota. Humphrey was also nominated by acclamation.

Citizens in one state in the Union were not allowed to vote for Johnson in the 1964 presidential election. What state was that?

Alabama. In that Southern state Johnson's name did not appear on the ballot, and write-in votes for him were not counted. Senator Barry Goldwater of Arizona, the Republican nominee, was listed on the Alabama ballot, and so was a group of "un-pledged" electors who also supported Goldwater.

Even though Goldwater carried Alabama by a margin of 689,818 votes to 0, he ran a poor race throughout most of the country and was badly defeated by Johnson. (See page 149 for the 1964 election results.)

The early primary election in the small state of New Hampshire had enormous repercussions in the campaign for the 1968 Democratic presidential nomination. Why was this so?

Despite the Johnson administration's steep escalation of the Vietnam War and its consequent unpopularity with the American public, most political pundits predicted that the President would run for and win renomination for another term in the White House. But Senator Eugene McCarthy of Minnesota, an out-spoken foe of the Vietnam War, entered the New Hampshire Democratic primary against a write-in delegation pledged to President Johnson's reelection. Johnson won the primary, but McCarthy garnered an astounding 42 percent of the total vote.

The Johnson supporters (and probably the President himself) were shocked by McCarthy's strong showing in New Hampshire. Less than three weeks later President Johnson changed the whole course of the 1968 campaign when he concluded a TV address by saying that he would not seek or accept another term because of "the divisiveness among us all tonight." The following Tuesday McCarthy again embarrassed Johnson by soundly thrashing him in the Wisconsin primary. This was next door to McCarthy's home state, but, even so, the incumbent President barely polled a scant one-third of the vote.

The other significant development caused by the New Hampshire primary was that it launched the late entry into the presidential race of Senator Robert Kennedy of New York, the younger brother of the slain President. Like McCarthy, Kennedy was a "dove" who opposed the Vietnam War.

After Robert Kennedy entered the race, were the votes of the antiwar protesters in state primaries divided between him and Eugene McCarthy?

Yes. After the Wisconsin primary election, McCarthy won in the next two states, Pennsylvania and Massachusetts, where Kennedy was only a write-in candidate. But once Kennedy's name appeared on the ballot, he defeated McCarthy by large margins in Indiana and Nebraska. McCarthy bounced back to win a narrow victory in Oregon in late May. The following week came the most important contest for delegates to the convention—the primary in heavily populated California.

Both McCarthy and Kennedy realized that whoever won in California would be the chief candidate of the "doves" at the convention. Their supporters waged a strenuous campaign in that large Western state, and over three million Democrats trooped to the polls in this crucial primary election. Kennedy carried the state by about 150,000 votes; it now appeared that he might be unstoppable in his quest for the Democratic nomination for President.

What tragic event on the night of Robert Kennedy's greatest triumph altered the course of the 1968 presidential campaign?

During the celebration of his victory in California (he also won that day in South Dakota), Robert Kennedy was assassinated in the kitchen of the Ambassador Hotel in Los Angeles.

Why did Vice-President Hubert Humphrey enter the race for the Democratic presidential nomination in 1968?

After Johnson pulled out of the race, his supporters turned to Humphrey as the President's replacement. The Vice-President was widely known and respected. He was liberal on domestic issues and loyal to the President in the controversy over the Vietnam War. Moreover, Humphrey had earned a reputation as a strong, effective speaker and a tireless campaigner.

The Vice-President stayed out of the primaries and depended on state organizations, favorite sons, and party bosses to prevent the Kennedy-McCarthy forces from lining up enough delegates to nominate a peace candidate. Senators Walter Mondale of Minnesota and Fred Harris of Oklahoma were Humphrey's campaign managers.

Why has the Democratic convention in 1968 been called the ugliest and most violent convention in our history?

Members of the Youth International Party (the "Yippies") and the National Mobilization Committee to End the War, along with other antiwar dissidents, assembled at Chicago, hoping to stage huge demonstrations and, if possible, to disrupt the convention proceedings. Anticipating trouble from the protesters, Mayor Richard J. Daley put Chicago's 12,000 police on 12-hour shifts, and thousands of national guardsmen and federal troops were stationed nearby. The dissidents were denied permission to parade and ordered to disperse when they attempted to camp in a park.

On the third night of the convention, while nominating and balloting for President were taking place inside the hall, the police confronted the jeering protesters with clubs. They viciously mauled many demonstrators and also some innocent bystanders in the crowd.

Inside the convention hall, did the biggest battle occur over the nomination of the presidential candidate?

No. Humphrey was an easy winner on the first ballot, amassing 1,759¼ votes to 601 for McCarthy, the closest runner-up.

The most heated battle in the convention came when the Democrats fought over the plank in their party platform about the Vietnam War. The Humphrey supporters generally favored the administration's policies in the war, supported a bombing halt against enemy positions only when it "would not endanger our troops in the field," and did not call for a withdrawal of United States military forces until after the war was successfully concluded. The "doves," on the other hand, demanded an immediate halt to the bombing, negotiations for a mutual withdrawal of United States and North Vietnamese troops, and encouragement of the South Vietnamese government to reach a peaceful settlement with the Communist forces.

More than 30 speakers addressed the convention on the war issue, and the heated debate continued for many hours. Finally, when the vote was taken, the pro-war side won by a margin of 1,567¾ to 1,041¼.

What Republican was given a second chance to win the presidency in 1968?

Former Vice-President Richard Nixon, who had lost the presidential race to John F. Kennedy in 1960 and the gubernatorial election in California to Governor Edmund G. Brown in 1962.

In 1968 the vice-presidential nominees of the two major parties came from families whose names had been Marciszewski and

Anagnostopoulous. The American public knew these men by what names?

The Democratic vice-presidential nominee was Maine Senator Edmund S. Muskie, whose family came to the United States from Poland, and his Republican opponent was Maryland Governor Spiro T. Agnew, whose family was of Greek origin.

What former governor ran a strong race on a third-party ticket in 1968?

Former Alabama Governor George C. Wallace of Alabama, who was the presidential candidate of his personally created American Independent Party. Wallace appealed both to segregationists in the South and to many blue-collar workers across the country. He advocated states' rights and "law and order," while opposing Washington bureaucrats, civil rights militants, school busing, and the liberal decisions of the Supreme Court.

Why did Humphrey face an uphill struggle in the 1968 campaign?

Humphrey presided over a badly divided Democratic Party. Many in the conservative wing of the party would vote for Wallace instead. An even more serious problem for Humphrey was the Vietnam War issue, which hung like an albatross around his neck. Most war protesters found it impossible to support the Vice-President as long as he supported the conflict in Asia.

By October it was clear that Humphrey could not win back Democratic dissidents unless he committed himself to ending all United States bombing in Vietnam. So in the last few weeks of the campaign, the old pro from Minnesota took a more compromising position on this thorny question. But Humphrey did not emerge from the Vietnam quagmire until just before the election when President Johnson announced an unconditional bombing halt.

Nixon had a comfortable lead over Humphrey in the polls in early autumn, but the Vice-President's campaign finally caught fire in the final days of October. Humphrey greatly narrowed the gap and nearly—but not quite—overtook Nixon on election day. (See pages 161 and 162 for the 1968 election results.)

Four years later, in 1972, who was considered the front-runner for the Democratic presidential nomination?

Maine Senator Edmund S. Muskie. The tall, craggy-faced Muskie had made a favorable impression on many voters when he was Humphrey's running mate in 1968. Moreover, the poll-sters showed Muskie running well against President Nixon in trial heats. In the spring of 1971 a Harris Poll found Muskie ahead of Nixon 47 to 39 percent.

It was thought that Muskie's chief rivals for the top spot on the Democratic ticket in 1972 would be Humphrey (whom Minnesota voters had returned to the Senate in 1970), Wallace (whom Alabama voters had returned to the statehouse in 1970), Senator Edward Kennedy of Massachusetts (who had dropped out of the race in January 1971), and Senator Henry M. Jackson of Washington. Several other Democrats tossed their hats into the ring, but they all were long-shot candidates and given little chance to win the nomination. One of these long shots was Senator George McGovern of South Dakota. A Gallup Poll in January 1972—only two months before the first state primary election—showed that McGovern was the favorite candidate of just 3 percent of the Democrats.

Muskie was both a winner and a loser in the first 1972 primary election in New Hampshire. How was this possible?

Muskie actually won the New Hampshire primary (just as Lyndon B. Johnson had done in 1968) with 46 percent of the vote. But a long-shot candidate (just as Eugene McCarthy had been in 1968) stunned all the politicians by capturing a sur-prisingly large share of the vote. This long-shot candidate was McGovern, whose 37 percent of the vote staggered the Muskie supporters, especially since New Hampshire borders the home state of the Maine senator.

What was George McGovern's appeal to the Democratic voters?

Senator McGovern, who had earned a Ph.D at Northwestern University and taught history and political science at Dakota Wesleyan, was one of the first public figures to denounce Presi-dent Johnson's Vietnam policies. He argued that the government of South Vietnam was corrupt, ineffective, and unpopular with the Vietnamese people and that the United States should with-draw all its armed forces from that battle-scarred country.

McGovern took a liberal stance on other issues in 1972, in-cluding cuts in military spending, tax reform, favoritism to big business in the Nixon administration, an extension of minority and women's rights, more government jobs for the unemployed, and additional federal aid to the poor and handicapped people in American society.

Why did McGovern decide to enter many primary elections in 1972?

One reason was to get wider public exposure and show the party chieftains that he had strong support from the Democratic rank and file. Also, the primary route had now become the most likely road to the presidential nomination. In 1968 there had been only 17 state primaries, and they provided only 41 percent of the convention delegates. In 1972 there were 23 primary elections, which produced 63 percent—nearly two-thirds—of the delegates who would select the next Democratic nominee for President.

McGovern did not win all of the primaries he entered. He lost in three Southern states and in Maryland and Michigan to George Wallace, and in Pennsylvania, Indiana, and Ohio to Hubert Humphrey. But the South Dakota senator was victorious in eight primaries, including a hard-fought race against Humphrey in California.

Who was the first black woman to run for President?

Congresswoman Shirley Chisholm of New York was a Democratic candidate for the presidency in 1972. She won more than one-half million votes in the various primaries and carried New Jersey with two-thirds of the total primary vote. On the first convention ballot she received 151.95 votes.

What groups gained much larger representation at the 1972 Democratic convention?

Because of significant changes in the rules governing the distribution of seats, there were dramatic increases in the number of women, youth, and blacks at the 1972 convention. The number of women delegates rose from 13 percent in 1968 to 40 percent in 1972. The proportion of delegates under the age of 30 skyrocketed from 2.6 percent in 1968 to 21 percent four years later. The number of black delegates nearly tripled between 1968, when there were only 5.5 percent, and 1972, when there were 15 percent.

Was McGovern nominated on the first ballot at the 1972 convention?

Yes. On the first roll call McGovern received 1,715.35 votes, which was about 200 more than he needed for the nomination. Humphrey and Muskie dropped out of the race before the balloting began, and Jackson finished in second place with 534 votes, followed by Wallace with 385.7.

Senator Thomas Eagleton of Missouri was selected as McGovern's running mate.

Why was Eagleton later dropped from the Democratic ticket?

Shortly after the convention the media learned that Senator Eagleton had been hospitalized for mental illness three times and had received electroshock treatments at least twice. The disclosure of this startling news immediately raised the question of whether Eagleton had the emotional stability to handle the stressful duties required of a President, in case McGovern might be elected and then die in office.

At first McGovern told the press he was backing Eagleton "1,000 percent." But after a chorus of party leaders and editorial writers warned that Eagleton's health was a major concern to the voters, McGovern changed his mind and persuaded the Missouri senator to withdraw in the interest of party harmony.

Even after Eagleton stepped down, this episode continued to plague McGovern and reduced his chances of winning the presidency. Later he confessed that his handling of the Eagleton affair "convicted me of incompetence, vacillation, dishonesty, and cold calculation."

Who replaced Eagleton as McGovern's running mate?

McGovern desperately searched for a new vice-presidential candidate. He approached several prominent Democrats, including Senators Humphrey, Kennedy, and Muskie, but they all turned him down. Finally, he found Eagleton's replacement—R. Sargent Shriver, the United States ambassador to France, who was a Kennedy in-law and the former director of the Peace Corps. The Democratic National Committee held a special meeting to nominate Shriver formally.

In June 1972 burglars linked to Republican campaign leaders broke into the Democratic headquarters in the Watergate building.

Didn't this event boost McGovern's chances to defeat Nixon?

No. Although the press reported the Watergate break-in, the public did not realize until many months later that this sordid affair and its subsequent cover-up involved high officials in the White House.

With the enormous implications of Watergate still a closely guarded secret, Nixon won reelection by a landslide. (See page 167 for the 1972 election results.)

By the time of the next presidential campaign, in 1976, the American public had been fully informed about the Watergate affair. Why did this shocking episode especially help Jimmy Carter in his bid for the Democratic presidential nomination?

Because of Watergate, large numbers of Americans were disgusted with Republicans in particular and Washington officeholders in general. Most of the Democrats who sought the presidential nomination in 1976 were senators and congressmen—Washington insiders. Jimmy Carter, on the other hand, had never held an office in Washington. He was an outsider, a humble peanut farmer ready, willing, and able to do battle with the crooks and the cronies in our nation's tarnished capital. Carter's clean-living image, oft-repeated platitudes, strong spiritual convictions, and concern for the blacks and the poor at home and those deprived of human rights abroad all served to cast him as a noble knight in the minds of many voters.

What was Carter's strategy to win the top spot on the Democratic ticket?

Starting far behind his much-better-known rivals (as George McGovern had done four years before), Carter knew that he had to acquire broad-based support. He had to prove that a candidate from the Deep South could win in the North and appeal to both rural areas and large cities, blue-collar and white-collar workers, Catholics and Protestants, minorities and whites.

First he wanted to gain national attention by doing well in the early Iowa caucuses and the New Hampshire primary. Then he wanted to return below the Mason-Dixon line and knock out his strongest Southern rival, Governor George Wallace of Alabama, in Florida. Next he needed to win in big industrial states, such as Illinois and Pennsylvania. To climax his quest for convention votes, he would drive his triumphant bandwagon on a transcontinental trek that would sweep up the remaining votes in the states that had late primaries.

How well did Carter's strategy succeed?

He defeated his nearest rival in the Iowa caucuses by a two-to-one margin, thus raising the question among many voters, "Who is Jimmy Carter?" He led seven other major opponents (with 28 percent of the vote) in the New Hampshire primary, which resulted in his picture appearing on the covers of both *Time* and *Newsweek*.

The next week Carter finished fourth to Senator Henry M. Jackson of Washington in Massachusetts, but one week later he regained the role of front-runner by beating Wallace in Florida. Then came a string of victories in six states, including the large ones of Illinois and Pennsylvania.

Carter now was clearly on top and headed for almost certain nomination. But in the last few weeks of the primary season, his bandwagon sputtered rather than sped across the finish line. Between May 11 and the final primaries on June 8, Carter lost in Nebraska, Idaho, Oregon, and Montana to Senator Frank Church of Idaho and in Maryland, Nevada, and California to Governor Edmund G. Brown, Jr., of California. But during this same period Carter won seven states, and his victories in New Jersey and Ohio on the last day of the primaries assured him the nomination on the first ballot.

The runner-up to Carter in the race for the presidential nomination had not won in a single state primary. Who was he?

Arizona Congressman Morris K. Udall, who won 329½ votes to Carter's 2,238½. California Governor Edmund G. Brown, Jr., finished third with 300½ votes.

When Carter appeared before the convention to accept his nomination, his first words were the same ones he had used many times at the beginning of campaign speeches in places where he was not well known. What were these words?

"My name is Jimmy Carter, and I'm running for President."

What seven men did Carter personally interview before selecting his running mate?

Senators Walter F. Mondale of Minnesota, Edmund S. Muskie of Maine, John Glenn of Ohio, Henry M. Jackson of Washington, Frank Church of Idaho, Adlai E. Stevenson III of Illinois and Congressman Peter W. Rodino, Jr., of New Jersey. Mondale was Carter's first choice, and the convention nominated him.

Who was the first black woman to be a keynote speaker at a convention of either major party?

On the first night of the 1976 Democratic convention, keynote addresses were given by Barbara Jordan, a black congresswoman from Texas, and former astronaut Senator John Glenn of Ohio.

How did it happen that Gerald R. Ford, Carter's Republican rival in 1976, was our only President who never had been elected to either the presidency or the vice-presidency?

When Vice-President Spiro Agnew resigned from his office in 1973 under a cloud of corruption charges, President Richard Nixon appointed Congressman Gerald R. Ford of Michigan to fill the vacancy. The following year President Nixon himself resigned because of his role in the Watergate cover-up, and Ford was then elevated to the presidency.

What action taken by President Ford during his administration probably hurt his candidacy in 1976 more than any other single event?

On September 8, 1974, President Ford granted an unconditional pardon to former President Nixon in regard to any criminal charges that might arise from Nixon's involvement in Watergate.

Were there televised debates between the presidential candidates in the elections of 1964, 1968, and 1972?

No. After the four debates between Kennedy and Nixon in 1960, this campaign activity was suspended in the next three presidential elections because each time the leading candidate felt he had more to lose than to gain by debating his opponent. Lyndon B. Johnson in 1964 and Richard Nixon in 1968 and 1972 had sizable leads over their rivals and didn't want to jeopardize their front-running positions by unpredictable confrontations before national audiences.

Since Gerald Ford was an incumbent President in 1976, why did he want to debate challenger Jimmy Carter?

Unlike President Johnson in 1964 and President Nixon in 1972, President Ford was far behind his opponent in the polls when the 1976 campaign started. So Ford felt he had nothing to lose—and perhaps much to gain—by debating Carter.

Who was judged the winner of the Ford-Carter debates?

Pollsters measured public reaction after each of the three televised debates. They concluded that Ford had a slight edge in the first encounter and that Carter had won the last two. The only serious blunder made by either candidate occurred during the second debate when Ford mistakenly said, "There is no Soviet domination of Eastern Europe."

When was the first televised debate between vice-presidential candidates?

In 1976, when there was a single debate between the Democratic nominee, Senator Walter F. Mondale of Minnesota, and his Republican rival, Senator Robert Dole of Kansas. Political observers generally believed that Mondale gave a better performance than Dole.

Did blacks and other minorities play a large role in helping Carter defeat Ford in 1976?

Yes. In this close election more white people voted for Ford, but blacks and other minorities supported the Georgian by such huge margins that Carter was sent to the White House. Carter carried nearly the entire South, most of the industrial Northeast, and enough of the Midwest to give him—although only barely—the electoral votes needed to become the 39th President. (See pages 158 and 159 for the 1976 election results.)

Before Carter's election, who was the last candidate from the Deep South to be elected President?

Zachary Taylor of Louisiana, in 1848.

PURSUIT OF THE PRESIDENTIAL NOMINATION, 1980

Who were the three contenders for the Democratic presidential nomination in 1980?

President Jimmy Carter, who was seeking a second term in the White House, Senator Edward M. "Ted" Kennedy of Massachusetts, and Governor Edmund G. "Jerry" Brown, Jr., of California.

Which of these three candidates had been defeated the first time he ran for governor of his state?

In 1966 Carter was defeated for the Democratic gubernatorial nomination in Georgia by an arch-segregationist, Lester B. Maddox, who went on to crush his Republican rival in the general election.

In 1970, when Carter tried again to become governor of Georgia, did he succeed?

Yes.

Why wasn't Carter reelected to a second term as governor of Georgia?

Georgia law prohibits a governor from serving two terms in succession. So in 1975 Carter found himself without a government office, and almost immediately he plunged into his campaign for the presidency in 1976.

Which of the 1980 presidential aspirants had trained to be a Jesuit priest?

Jerry Brown, who entered the Jesuits' Sacred Heart Novitiate in 1956 but dropped out in 1960 after he decided not to become a priest.

What high government job had Jerry Brown's father held?

Edmund G. "Pat" Brown, Sr., was governor of California for two terms until he was defeated by Ronald Reagan in 1966.

How old was Ted Kennedy when he was first elected to the Senate in 1962?

He was just 30, which the Constitution decrees is the minimum age for a senator.

What personal tragedies played a large role in preventing Kennedy from running for the presidency before 1980?

The assassinations of two elder brothers made Ted Kennedy reluctant to expose himself to the heightened dangers that would surround his presidential candidacy. As the only surviving son, he became the surrogate father of his brothers' 13 children. His mother especially did not want Ted to risk his life in a presidential race.

Also, one night in 1969, Ted Kennedy had been at the wheel of a car that plunged off a bridge on Chappaquiddick Island, Massachusetts, and the accident resulted in the death of his woman companion. Many people concluded from this highly publicized incident that the woman's death was due to Kennedy's recklessness and negligence and that the senator had been callously irresponsible in not reporting the accident until many hours after it had occurred.

Another factor that made Kennedy shy away from running for the presidency was that his estranged wife suffered from emotional and alcoholic problems, and their marriage was in jeopardy of being terminated.

What did Kennedy say was his family's attitude about his entering the 1980 presidential race?

In the fall of 1979 Ted Kennedy announced that his family, including his mother and wife, had agreed to support whatever decision he made about running for President.

How did the polls affect Kennedy's decision to seek the White House in 1980?

Polls in the summer and fall of 1979 showed that Kennedy would be a much stronger Democratic candidate than Carter against Ronald Reagan or any other Republican nominee. Ironically, in the same week that Kennedy announced his candidacy, a dramatic event occurred that changed the entire course of the 1980 presidential campaign—sixty-six Americans were taken hostage in Teheran by the new Iranian government. Fourteen were released, but the others were held in captivity for more than a year.

When the hostages were first seized, Carter's popularity rose sharply and Kennedy's declined, chiefly because Americans tend to rally around their President during times of foreign crisis. But as month after month dragged by with Carter unable to secure the hostages' release, the President's popularity slipped lower and lower.

Why did both Ted Kennedy and Jerry Brown believe they had a chance to win the Democratic nomination from President Carter?

They felt that Carter was an inept leader who had not dealt effectively with serious economic problems, such as rising inflation and interest rates, or with critical foreign affairs, such as the Soviet invasion of Afghanistan in December 1979 and the hostages' incarceration in Iran.

Did Jerry Brown win any of the state primaries?

No. In all of the primaries that he entered Brown trailed both Carter and Kennedy (except in Michigan, where he trailed an unpledged delegation), and he dropped out of the race on April 1, 1980.

In how many state primaries was Kennedy victorious?

Kennedy carried only nine states and the District of Columbia. But in his column were some of the biggest states, including California, New York, Pennsylvania, and New Jersey.

Did Carter enter the convention with enough pledged delegates to assure his nomination?

Yes. Carter won 24 of the primaries and most of the delegates from states that selected their slates in caucuses. By the time that the convention assembled, he had gathered enough delegates to capture the nomination by a margin of about 315 votes.

What last-ditch effort did the Kennedy supporters make to try to prevent Carter's nomination?

The Kennedy camp, claiming that conditions had changed since the delegates had been elected months before, tried to overturn a convention rule that bound delegates to vote on the first ballot for the candidate to whom they had been pledged. Kennedy supporters argued vehemently that many delegates would vote for their man if they were released to "vote their own consciences." The debate on setting aside this rule provided the most fireworks at the convention, but when the issue was put to a vote Kennedy's motion was defeated by a vote of 1,936.418 to 1,390.580.

When the balloting for the presidential nomination took place, Carter won with 2,123 votes to Kennedy's 1,150.5. Vice-President Walter F. Mondale was also nominated for a second term.

When Carter finished his acceptance speech, did Kennedy join him on the platform with the other chieftains of the Democratic Party?

Yes, but Kennedy's appearance on the platform with Carter was very brief, and, grim-faced, he stiffly shook the President's hand. But he refrained from raising Carter's arm in the traditional victory salute. An embarrassed Carter watched disconsolately as his Democratic rival swiftly stalked off the platform. This brief episode reminded television viewers across the nation that the Democratic Party was badly divided as it faced the difficult task of trying to return Jimmy Carter to the White House.

The President had his work cut out for him. He was matched against the most charismatic Republican nominee since Eisenhower—former Governor Ronald Reagan of California. To make matters worse, a highly articulate liberal Republican congressman, John Anderson of Illinois, was running as an independent candidate, and he was certain to woo many voters away from the beleaguered President.

BATTLE FOR
THE WHITE HOUSE, 1980

When the 1980 battle for the White House was waged, why didn't Carter have a strong advantage over his challengers, since he already was President and had acquired four years of experience in the office?

Many voters perceived Carter as Kennedy and Brown did in the primaries and as Reagan and Anderson did in the general election: they considered him a weak President whose domestic and foreign policies were inconsistent and generally unsuccessful. When pollsters asked the American people in 1980 how they assessed Carter's performance as President, he received lower marks than those of any Chief Executive since this question was first asked by poll-takers in President Truman's administration.

What campaign charges did Carter make against Reagan?

Carter tried to portray Reagan as the most extreme right-winger to run for the presidency since Barry Goldwater was the Republican nominee in 1964. He also implied that the actor-turned-politician lacked experience in dealing with the intricacies of foreign and domestic issues and offered simplistic answers to complex questions.

Undoubtedly Carter's most effective charge, especially with women voters, was that Reagan's views on foreign affairs were strident and bellicose and might precipitate war. On the domestic front, the President contended that his Republican opponent would favor the rich over the middle class and the poor, reverse social welfare programs (possibly crippling Social Security), and call a halt to the progress that was being made in civil rights and women's rights.

What role did former President Gerald Ford play in helping the Republican cause in 1980?

Between Labor Day and election day on November 4, Ford campaigned 53 of the 64 days, covering 30 states and about 60,000 miles. No other former GOP President ever traveled so far or made so many public appearances in behalf of other Republican candidates.

Ford attacked Carter on three economic issues that affected millions of American families. What were these issues?

Inflation, unemployment, and interest rates. Ford said that when he left the White House inflation had been 4.8 percent but that under Carter's presidency it had risen to nearly 13 percent. "Unemployment in my home state of Michigan in the auto industry," Ford asserted, "is over 15 percent, almost as bad as it was during the Great Depression." Moreover, interest rates had soared to record heights. The former President concluded that Carter "was handed the economy on a silver platter, and he blew it."

During the campaign Reagan repeatedly called for increased defense spending. Why did he believe that this offered the best hope for preserving peace with the Soviet Union?

Reagan asserted that if the United States spent enough money on defense to achieve a "margin of safety" in strategic weapons, the Soviet Union would not dare to challenge it militarily. On the other hand, the failure of our nation to keep pace with Soviet weapons was a serious threat to peace, said Reagan, because it would encourage Soviet expansion and "could back us into war."

How much money did Carter and Reagan receive from the federal government to help finance their political campaigns?

They each received about $29.4 million of federal funds for the general election campaign.

Were the presidential campaigns limited to federal financing?

No. The Supreme Court ruled that independent groups could raise and spend money for a presidential election, as long as there was no direct collaboration between these political groups and the candidate or his advisers. This court ruling triggered the growth of many political-action committees (PACs), which helped finance the campaigns of their candidates.

In what areas that usually are heavily Democratic did Reagan campaign vigorously?

Reagan carried his campaign into the heartland of industrial America, from the automobile assembly lines in Michigan to the steel plants in Ohio, the coal mines in Pennsylvania, and the garment factories in New York. He waged a more intense effort to win blue-collar support than did any other GOP presidential candidate in this century.

The Republican nominee also refused to concede the South to the former peanut farmer from Georgia, and Reagan spoke at many rallies south of the Mason-Dixon line.

What issues did Reagan stress when he appealed for the blue-collar vote?

He emphasized the pocketbook issues—spiraling inflation and interest rates and growing unemployment. Reagan also stressed his concern about our weakening military posture compared to that of the Soviets and our declining role in world affairs. He also impressed many workers with his plea for a stronger enforcement of law and order, a renewed commitment to traditional family values, and his opposition to abortion.

Did Reagan win the endorsement of any large unions?

Yes, both the huge Teamsters Union and the National Maritime Union supported the Republican candidate.

What Democratic leader of the "doves" in the Vietnam War announced his support for Reagan?

Eugene McCarthy, the former senator from Minnesota, who was one of the chief leaders in the protest against the Vietnam War.

On the eve of the one Carter-Reagan debate, did it appear that the presidential race was close?

Yes. By late October the chief polls showed that Reagan and Carter were running "neck and neck," and some public opinion surveys gave Carter a slight lead. It appeared that Carter was gaining more support, primarily among women voters, by his often-repeated claims that Reagan favored a dangerous arms race with the Soviet Union and was weak on the issue of preserving peace.

Was Carter or Reagan considered the "winner" of their debate?

This single television confrontation before over 100 million Americans, exactly one week before the election, was judged a draw by some debate experts, but polls soon revealed that the majority of TV viewers were much more favorably impressed by Reagan's performance than by Carter's.

What factors caused Reagan to "win" the debate in the eyes of the public?

First and foremost, Reagan effectively answered the war-and-peace issue that had concerned millions of voters. "I'm here to tell you," he declared, "that I believe with all my heart that our first priority must be world peace, and that the use of force is always and only a last resort." The GOP nominee also attacked the Carter economic record, reminding the viewers of the high levels of taxation, inflation, interest rates, and unemployment.

More subtly, but perhaps more important to the huge TV audience, Reagan portrayed the image of a warm, friendly man with a strong capacity for leadership and a positive, hopeful approach to the serious problems Americans faced.

Carter, by contrast, was put on the defensive, and he appeared somber, taut, and somewhat strident and scolding. But the rather ill-at-ease President was matched against a master TV performer; it has often been said that former actor Reagan uses television more effectively than any other politician since the birth of this medium.

How did the frustrating issue of the American hostages held in Iran affect the election?

Republican leaders admitted that if the hostages came home

just before the election, this dramatic event could be interpreted as a major diplomatic triumph for the President, and it might swing a grateful electorate to Carter. The Sunday before the election the Iranian parliament finally voted to free the American captives, but only if the United States would comply with four specific demands.

However, this apparent break in the lengthy impasse with Iran did not produce an immediate release of the hostages—which was needed to boost Carter's chances for reelection. Instead, the news from Iran seemed to remind voters that election day would occur exactly one year after the hostages had been seized, and during that long year of anguished waiting for their safe return, the President had been powerless to secure their release. So many voters viewed the hostage issue as an example of Carter's inability to assert strong, successful leadership.

What role did the fundamentalist religious groups play in the 1980 election?

In 1976 many Protestant fundamentalists supported "born-again" Baptist Jimmy Carter. But in 1980 large numbers of them voted Republican because they preferred the GOP positions on such issues as abortion, the Equal Rights Amendment, school prayers and busing, national defense, and government spending. Moreover, religious activist groups such as the Moral Majority registered perhaps as many as four million new voters in the hope they would cast their ballots for Reagan and other Republican conservatives.

On the final weekend before the election, what were the pollsters predicting?

Many pollsters felt the election would be very close, with Reagan only a slight favorite to win. *Time* and *Newsweek* surveys showed Carter narrowly ahead in the popular vote but substantially behind in the all-important electoral vote. CBS News/*New York Times* gave Reagan the popular-vote lead at 44 to 43 percent, and the final Gallup Poll showed Reagan ahead 47 to 44 percent. The only poll that suggested a larger Republican victory was the ABC News/Harris Survey, but even its 45-to-40-percent forecast was much smaller than the size of Reagan's victory on election day.

Why did the polls fail to detect the Reagan landslide?

Until the last few days of the campaign there were unusually large numbers of undecided voters and people who leaned slightly toward Carter. Apparently many of these voters made up their minds to cast Republican ballots during the week before the election. The pollsters did not accurately forecast the size of the dramatic shift in voters' sentiments partly because it continued to snowball in the final days, even hours, before the election.

How large was Reagan's landslide victory?

The Republican candidate won all but six states and the District of Columbia. His winning margins in both the popular and electoral votes were huge.

	Popular vote	%	Electoral votes	%
Ronald Reagan (R)	43,904,153	50.7	489	91
Jimmy Carter (D)	35,483,883	41.0	49	9
John Anderson (I)	5,720,060	6.6	0	0
Other candidates	1,407,125	1.7	0	0

Who was the last Democratic President before Carter to lose an election for a second term?

Grover Cleveland, who lost his bid for reelection in 1888.

Who was the last elected President of either party to be defeated for reelection?

Herbert Hoover, in 1932. Ironically, the 1980 election results were remarkably similar to the 1932 election. The defeated candidates each won only six states and had about the same number of electoral votes (Carter 49, Hoover 59). Both elections also reflected dramatic philosophical changes among the voters: from conservative to liberal in 1932, from liberal to conservative in 1980.

Some Democratic leaders had predicted before the election that if Carter lost it would be mainly because Anderson took votes that would have gone to Carter in a two-way race. Were these predictions accurate?

Anderson's vote was larger than Reagan's margin of victory

in 14 states with a combined total of 158 electoral votes. But even if Carter had won all these 14 states, his electoral count would have totaled only 207, or 63 votes short of the number needed to win the election. And when pollsters asked Anderson voters as they left the precincts whom they would have favored in a two-way race, nearly half of them answered "Reagan." Also, the Anderson factor cut both ways. In four of the six states Carter carried, his margin of victory was smaller than the combined Reagan-Anderson vote total.

In his 1976 victory Carter's most solid base of support had been the South. What happened in the Southern states in the 1980 election?

Southerners overwhelmingly repudiated the first native son from the Deep South to occupy the White House since 1850. Whereas Carter had captured all of the states of the Old Confederacy except Virginia in 1976, he lost all of them except his home state of Georgia in 1980.

How many states did Reagan carry by more than a two-to-one margin?

Nine. These states were Alaska, Arizona, Idaho, Nebraska, Nevada, New Hampshire, North Dakota, Utah, and Wyoming.

What is the only state Reagan captured which no other Republican nominee had ever won, except Nixon in 1972?

Arkansas.

What state that had not voted Republican since Eisenhower's reelection in 1956 provided Reagan his narrowest victory margin?

Massachusetts, where less than 4,000 votes determined the winner.

	Reagan	Carter	Anderson
Massachusetts	1,057,631	1,053,802	382,539

What groups of voters gave Reagan his impressive victory at the polls?

Reagan drew his electoral strength from a wide cross section of the voting public in every region of the country. He was a big winner among males, whites, farmers, and Protestants. He carried the normally Democratic Catholic vote and an unusually large percentage of the Jewish vote. Reagan made deep inroads into the blue-collar and union vote, which any Democrat needs to win the presidency. Independents, the swing voters that both parties court, went to Reagan by more than a five-to-three margin. Even about one-third of the registered Democrats voted Republican in this election.

The only large Democratic groups who stayed overwhelmingly loyal to Carter were the blacks and Hispanics.

Did more people vote in 1980 than in any previous presidential election?

Yes. About 86.5 million Americans cast their ballots in 1980. This was nearly 5 million more voters than in 1976, the year with the second largest turnout.

Was the proportion of voters to the total adult population also larger in 1980 than in any previous presidential election?

No. The proportion of voters has declined in each of the last five presidential elections.

1960 . . . . 63.1%
1964 . . . . 61.8%
1968 . . . . 60.7%
1972 . . . . 55.4%
1976 . . . . 54.4%
1980 . . . . 53.2%

Not since 1948, when the voter turnout was only 51.1%, has there been a smaller proportion of voters to the adult population than there was in 1980.

Between 1900 and 1980 there were 21 presidential elections. Did Democrats or Republicans win more of these elections?

The Democrats and Republicans had the same number of victories going into the 1980 election, but Ronald Reagan's trimph in 1980 gave the GOP an 11-10 lead in presidential elections during the twentieth century.

PURSUIT OF THE
PRESIDENTIAL NOMINATION,
1984

On December 1, 1982, Senator Edward Kennedy of Massachusetts, then leading all other Democrats by a large margin in the polls, announced he would not seek the 1984 nomination. Which two Democrats emerged as the front runners in 1983?

Former Vice-President Walter F. Mondale and Ohio Senator John Glenn ran neck-and-neck in the polls during the summer of 1983, but toward the end of the year Glenn's campaign faltered. Although he earnestly presented a cluster of solutions to foreign and domestic problems, Glenn had trouble combining them into a credo that would give Democrats a clear reason for supporting him. Also, Glenn's campaign organization was weak, and the former astronaut was not an effective speaker.

There were eight major contenders for the 1984 Democratic presidential nomination. How many of them had ever served in the Senate?

Six. Four of the candidates were senators in 1984: Alan Cranston of California, John Glenn of Ohio, Gary Hart of Colorado, and Ernest F. Hollings of South Carolina. Two candidates were former senators: George McGovern of South Dakota (1963-1981) and Walter F. Mondale of Minnesota (1964-1976). The other two contenders were Reubin Askew, former governor of Florida (1971-1979), and Reverend Jesse Jackson of Chicago, Illinois.

Which of these candidates based his campaign primarily on the issue of a nuclear arms freeze?

Alan Cranston.

Only one of these candidates previously had been the Democratic nominee for President. Who is he?

George McGovern, who headed the Democratic ticket in 1972 and lost to Richard Nixon.

Which candidate was pursuing a career in religion until his interest was altered by volunteer service in Senator John F. Kennedy's 1960 presidential campaign?

Gary Hart, who had been a student at Yale Divinity School before the 1960 presidential election. After the election he enrolled in and later graduated from the Yale Law School.

Which candidate's famous achievement in 1962 was dramatized in a popular 1983 movie?

The Right Stuff told the story of John Glenn as the first American space pilot to orbit the earth.

One of the candidates gained nationwide attention from his successful mission to Syria in late 1983. Who is he?

Jesse Jackson. He helped gain the release of Navy flier Robert O. Goodman, who had been shot down over Syria.

Which candidate advocated an across-the-board freeze on federal spending that would affect all government-funded programs, from welfare services to national defense?

Ernest F. Hollings.

Which candidate spoke out strongly against abortion and favored nuclear deterrence instead of a nuclear freeze?

Reubin Askew.

Jesse Jackson's campaign theme was to help what he called the "rainbow coalition." Who is included in this coalition?

Groups in America with special needs, such as minorities, women, homosexuals, and poor people.

From 1960 to 1981 Walter F. Mondale served in state and national elective positions. When was the first time he ran for an office

in which he was not already the incumbent?

In 1976, when he ran for the vice-presidency. He had been appointed attorney general of Minnesota in 1960 and U.S. senator in 1964; he was reelected to both offices twice.

Why did the Democratic Party make it more difficult for a long shot to win the presidential nomination in 1984?

The party leaders felt they had been virtually ignored when "outsiders" George McGovern in 1972 and Jimmy Carter in 1976 came from far back in the pack to capture the presidential nomination. So in 1984 about 14 percent of the convention delegates were not elected in primaries or state caucuses. These "superdelegates" generally were national and state office-holders, who were awarded convention seats because of their prominence in the party.

Were there more Democratic primary elections in 1984 than there had been in 1980?

No, in 1984 there were 25 delegate selection primaries compared to 35 in 1980. Several states switched from primary elections to caucuses in 1984. This was another indication of restoring more power to party regulars, who usually play a larger role in caucuses than in primaries.

Before the first delegates were elected, why was Walter Mondale the heavy favorite to win the presidential nomination?

Mondale had put together an excellent campaign organization and collected more money than any of his rivals. Moreover, in October 1983 he had won the endorsement of the AFL-CIO, which was the first time that this large, powerful union had ever supported a candidate before the primary season began. Mondale also gained early endorsements from the National Education Association and the National Organization for Women.

Why were the endorsements by these huge organizations not entirely a blessing to Mondale?

They gave rise to the claim that Mondale was too closely tied to special interests and had "promised everything to everyone." In the Des Moines debate, one week before the Iowa caucuses, rival Gary Hart asked Mondale to name a single major policy disagreement he had with the AFL-CIO, and the former Vice-President did not answer the question directly.

Did Mondale win the nation's first caucuses in Iowa on February 20?

Yes, Mondale swept to an easy victory, garnering 49 percent of the vote. This was about triple the 16.5 percent gained by Hart, the surprise runner-up. Glenn finished a disappointing sixth, capturing less than 4 percent of the vote.

The following week New Hampshire held the first primary, and a few days later Democrats voted in Maine and Vermont. How did these three early elections abruptly change the direction of the race for the presidential nomination?

In New Hampshire Hart scored a stunning upset, winning over 37 percent of the vote to Mondale's 28 percent. Then Hart scored a decisive victory in the Maine caucuses, and he overwhelmed Mondale in Vermont's nonbinding primary, 71 to 21 percent. Mondale's hope of winning the presidential nomination easily had now been dashed, and he no longer was the acknowledged front-runner.

Why was Hart's sudden success considered so astonishing?

Less than a month before New Hampshire's primary on February 28, polls showed that Hart was the favorite candidate of a mere 3 to 5 percent of Democrats nationwide. But in March, shortly after Hart's first three triumphs in New England, a Gallup Poll revealed that his popularity had skyrocketed to the point that he even led Ronald Reagan in the presidential race, 52 to 43 percent, while Mondale trailed the President, 45 to 50 percent. Never before had any long-shot candidate for the White House soared so high so fast.

What factors accounted for Hart's appeal to many voters?

Hart campaigned on the vibrant theme that he could bring to the nation "new ideas and new leadership." He portrayed Mondale as a captive of the Establishment, which was tied to old-fashioned, unsuccessful policies of the past. Hart's youthful vigor, rugged good looks, and dramatic mannerisms reminded many voters of a popular former President, John F. Kennedy.

Why was March 13 called "Super Tuesday"?

Because on that day Democrats selected 505 convention delegates (more than one eighth of the total number) in nine states, five with primaries and four with caucuses.

Was there a clearcut winner on "Super Tuesday"?

No. Hart carried six states, including Florida and Massachusetts. But Mondale slowed the momentum of his spectacular rival by defeating him in Alabama and Georgia and running second to an unpledged delegation in Hawaii. Had Mondale failed to capture any of the nine states, his prospect of winning the nomination would have been very bleak.

After "Super Tuesday" how many of the eight Democratic presidential candidates were still in the race?

Only three—Mondale, Hart, and Jackson.

Mondale hit the comeback trail, and between March 14 and May 7 he won primaries or caucuses in the largest midwestern state, the two largest states in the East, and the largest southwestern state. Which states are these?

Illinois, New York, Pennsylvania, and Texas. During this same seven-week period Mondale captured eleven other states and Hart six.

What accounted for Mondale's new surge of strength at the polls?

The former Vice-President abandoned the complacent, restrained role that he had portrayed in the early stages of the campaign, rolled up his sleeves, and began counterattacking. He charged that Hart's "new ideas" lacked substance and criticized the Colorado senator for some of his stands on domestic and defense issues. Moreover, once the spotlight was focused on Hart, he had trouble articulating his views in a way that would sustain his campaign momentum.

By May 8 it appeared that Mondale had almost clinched the Democratic nomination. What happened that day which breathed new life into Hart's campaign?

Hart unexpectedly won the Ohio and Indiana primaries in the Midwest, the region where Mondale was strongest. These victories assured Hart that his campaign would stay alive until the ballots were counted in the final primaries on June 5.

Who won the June 5 elections that marked the end of the bitter, hard-fought struggle in primaries and caucuses throughout the nation?

The results were mixed. Hart won a lopsided victory in

California, the most populous state, and also carried South Dakota and New Mexico. Mondale took New Jersey by a huge margin and captured West Virginia.

When did Mondale finally claim victory in the race for the presidential nomination?

On June 6, the day after the final primary elections, Mondale claimed he had gone over the top and had more than the 1,967 delegates needed to win the nomination. The news services agreed that Mondale was the winner, but only by a slim margin. Later, many uncommitted Democrats, including Senator Edward M. Kennedy of Massachusetts, climbed on the Mondale bandwagon.

Did Mondale actually win more primaries than Hart?

No. Hart won twelve primaries to Mondale's eleven.

Did Jackson win any primaries or caucuses?

Yes, he won the primaries in Louisiana and the District of Columbia, and in the South Carolina caucuses he gained more delegates than either Mondale or Hart.

Although he did not gain many states, why was Jackson's campaign remarkable?

Jesse Jackson was the first black candidate in the history of American politics to wage a serious nationwide campaign for the presidential nomination. He inspired large numbers of blacks to register and vote (many for the first time), carried several big cities, including Chicago and Philadelphia, and picked up 367 delegates elected in primaries and caucuses.

Did Jackson play a significant role in prolonging Mondale's quest for the nomination?

Some political experts believe that if Jackson had not been in the race, Mondale would have fallen heir to most of the black vote and won the nomination much easier and earlier than he did. Other experts feel that Jackson created much of his own constituency and that many of his supporters would not have voted if he had not been a candidate.

Did Jackson's vote come almost entirely from blacks?

Yes. In some states Jackson won an enormous amount of the black vote (89 percent in New York, 74 percent in Illinois and Pennsylvania). But his dream of gaining widespread support from the "rainbow coalition" never caught hold, and in no state did he get as much as 10 percent of the white vote.

How did Jackson offend many Jews?

Jews were angered by Jackson's openly pro-Arab and anti-Israel remarks. Also, they were insulted by his private reference early in the campaign to Jews as "Hymies," and they felt Jackson waited too long to repudiate the anti-Semitism of Islam leader Louis Farrakhan, a strong Jackson supporter.

With what types of voters was Mondale most popular?

Union members, teachers, older people, longtime party workers, low income groups, and Hispanics.

With what types of voters was Hart most popular?

Young persons, college graduates, middle and high income groups, Democrats who had voted for Ronald Reagan in 1980, and independent voters.

Where was the 1984 Democratic convention, and when was the only other time that the Democrats met in this city?

San Francisco. The only other Democratic convention held in this city was in 1920 when the party nominated the losing ticket of James M. Cox for President and Franklin D. Roosevelt for Vice-President.

Before the Democratic convention opened, Walter Mondale announced that Congresswoman Geraldine Ferraro of New York would be his running mate. How many times in the past had the Democrat who was expected to win the presidential nomination named his running mate in advance of the convention?

None.

Geraldine Ferraro was the first woman ever nominated by either major party to run on a presidential ticket. Her nomination provided another historic breakthrough. What was it?

She was the first Democrat (or Republican) of Italian descent to run for President or Vice-President.

Since 1979 Ferraro represented what New York area in Congress?

The Queens section of New York City, which has often been called "Archie Bunker's district."

What other New Yorker thrilled the convention with his keynote address in which he attacked President Reagan's domestic and foreign policies?

Governor Mario Cuomo.

When was the last time that a Democratic convention failed to nominate its presidential candidate on the first ballot?

In 1952, when three ballots were needed to nominate Adlai Stevenson.

Was Walter Mondale nominated on the first ballot at the 1984 convention?

Yes. Mondale received 2,191 votes (224 more than was needed), Hart got 1,279.5 votes, and Jackson 465.5 votes.

Did Jackson and Hart make any efforts to unify the Democrats before the convention adjourned?

Yes. In an impassioned speech Jackson apologized for his remarks during the campaign that may have offended others and promised to support the Democratic ticket. Hart pledged to "devote every working hour and every ounce of energy to the defeat of Ronald Reagan," and when Mondale went over the top in the delegate count, Hart asked the convention to make the nomination unanimous.

Mondale was often called bland and more subdued than most politicians. Did his convention address in which he accepted the presidential nomination reflect these qualities?

No. The former Vice-President delivered a stirring speech in which he lashed out at many aspects of the Reagan administration and implored the voters to entrust their future to his leadership. His emotional rhetoric stirred the spirits of the assembled Democrats, but all of them knew that ahead lay an uphill struggle to unseat a popular President.

BATTLE FOR
THE WHITE HOUSE, 1984

Who was the last major candidate—Democrat or Republican—to announce his intentions to run for the presidency in 1984?

President Ronald Reagan, who entered the race on January 29, 1984. All of the eight major Democratic contenders had tossed their hats in the ring in 1983.

When the 1984 campaign began, why were Democrats encouraged by the large increase of voters in the 1982 congressional elections?

In 1982 the vote for Democratic House candidates increased by more than six million over the vote in 1978, the most recent previous midterm congressional election. The 1982 vote for Republican House candidates rose by only three million.

Why did the gender gap also encourage Democrats?

Women have cast more ballots than men in every presidential election since 1964, and it was thought that in 1984 several million more women than men might go to the polls. In the 1980 election men voters preferred Ronald Reagan to Jimmy Carter by 56 to 36 percent, but women gave Reagan only a bare 47-to-45 percent margin of their votes. Two years later, exit polls showed that women favored Democratic congressional candidates over Republicans by 21 percent, and in that same year women provided the margins that elected three new

Democratic governors—Mario Cuomo of New York, Mark White of Texas, and James Blanchard of Michigan.

Immediately after its convention a political party usually enjoys at least a temporary upward surge in the polls. Did this happen after the 1984 Democratic convention?

Yes. In a July 13-16 preconvention Gallup Poll Reagan led Mondale by 53 to 39 percent, but on July 20, the day after the Democratic convention adjourned, a new Gallup Poll showed that Mondale had taken a narrow 48-to-46 percent lead. A Harris survey also found the two tickets virtually tied in a poll taken during the five days after the convention. However, by July 30 Gallup reported that Reagan had regained his lead by a margin of 53 to 41 percent.

Traditionally, presidential candidates do little or no campaigning between the end of the conventions and Labor Day. Was this true also in 1984?

No. On July 25, less than a week after the Democratic convention and nearly a month before the Republican convention, President Reagan launched the opening salvo of his reelection campaign in Austin, Texas, charging that the Democratic leaders "have moved so far left, they've left America." Meanwhile, Walter Mondale and Geraldine Ferraro started campaigning on July 31 at Cleveland, Ohio, and then addressed rallies in Mississippi and Texas.

When the Republican convention met in Dallas, Texas, in August, it nominated Ronald Reagan for a second term by a nearly unanimous vote (two delegates abstained). When was the last time that an incumbent President won renomination without at least token opposition?

In 1956, when Dwight D. Eisenhower was nominated for a second term.

In August 1981, President Reagan signed into law two important economic bills that had major repercussions in his 1984 campaign for reelection. What did these laws do?

One law reduced government spending on domestic programs by $130 billion over three years. The other law cut taxes by $750 billion over three years.

Despite the large cuts in government spending for domestic programs, why did the federal budget deficit greatly increase during the Reagan administration?

The spiraling budget deficit was caused largely by a massive defense buildup to match the Soviet Union's military might, the large reduction in taxes, and the burgeoning interest that had to be paid on the growing deficit.

How did possible tax raises become a major campaign issue in 1984?

In his acceptance speech at the Democratic convention, Walter Mondale asserted that following the election taxes would have to be raised to reduce the deficit, but that President Reagan would not admit this to the American public. The President replied that he was strongly against raising taxes and would take such action "only as a last resort." The GOP platform declared even more emphatically that Republicans would "categorically reject proposals to increase taxes in a misguided effort to balance the budget."

In September Mondale unveiled his plan for lowering the deficit, which he estimated would shrink federal red ink by about two-thirds by 1989. What were the chief points of this plan?

Besides increasing personal income taxes for couples making more than $60,000 a year, Mondale called for modifying tax indexing (scheduled to begin in 1985) for couples earning more than $25,000 a year and a 15 percent minimum income tax on corporations. Mondale said he would also tighten rules on tax shelters and loopholes and set aside added revenues in a special fund for deficit reduction.

His spending cuts would include $51 billion in interest payments due to lower borrowing costs as the deficit shrinks and $25 billion by canceling some defense projects. Mondale also advocated saving on Medicare by capping medical costs and on agriculture by boosting farm exports.

How did Democrats and Republicans disagree about the domestic spending cuts in the Reagan administration?

Democrats charged that millions of Americans had been hurt by the scaling down of such government programs as food stamps, free school lunches, student loans, Aid to Families with

Dependent Children, Medicaid, and Social Security payments to disabled persons. Republicans responded that the nation had gone much too far in the direction of creating a welfare state, and the time had come to reverse this trend which had become very costly to the taxpayers.

What remarks made by Reagan at a Dallas prayer breakfast brought religion into the campaign?

Reagan declared that "religion and politics are necessarily related" and "this has worked to our benefit as a nation." These statements led Mondale to question whether the President believed in the separation of church and state. Mondale asserted that "most Americans would be surprised to learn that God is a Republican" and condemned what he called "the rise of moral McCarthyism."

How did Reagan respond to these charges?

While he praised a "new spiritual awareness" in the nation, the President declared that "the United States of America is, and must remain, a nation of openness to people of all beliefs . . . . The ideals of our country leave no room whatsoever for intolerance, anti-Semitism, or bigotry of any kind—none. The unique thing about America is a wall in our Constitution separating church and state."

How did the candidates differ on the question of prayer in schools?

Reagan said that one of the reasons for his decision to seek reelection was to advance "the need to bring God back into the schools." He supported a constitutional amendment permitting voluntary prayer in school and accused its opponents of being "intolerant of religion."

Mondale took the position that students can pray whenever they wish but there should be no organized prayer in classrooms. "A President," he said, "must not let it be thought that political dissent from him is un-Christian."

How did Reagan and Mondale disagree on the abortion issue?

Reagan supported the so-called right-to-life constitutional amendment to ban abortion, while Mondale opposed the amendment, saying that the decision on abortion "essentially has to be a judgment made by people in their own lives on the basis of their own faith."

What position did Geraldine Ferraro, a Catholic, take on abortion?

She personally opposed abortion but said her religious beliefs did not affect her conduct in public office and that she supported the 1973 Supreme Court decision permitting abortion. Her position was attacked by various Catholic clergymen and often led to protests by right-to-life supporters at her political rallies.

Did most evangelical fundamentalist Protestant groups, such as the Moral Majority, support Reagan in 1984?

Yes. They generally agreed with Reagan's views and vowed to register many new voters for the Republican cause. Mondale was concerned that these religious groups were "reaching for government power to impose their own beliefs on other people. And the Reagan administration has opened its arms to them."

Why was the future course of the Supreme Court an issue in the 1984 presidential election?

Five of the nine justices were 75 or older, so there was a strong likelihood that the man elected to the White House in 1984 would be filling several vacancies on the Supreme Court.

Revelations about the finances of Geraldine Ferraro and her husband, John Zaccaro, undoubtedly hurt the Democrats' cause. Who was the last previous vice-presidential candidate to have his finances questioned?

Richard Nixon, whose contributions from wealthy constituents led to his famous "Checkers" speech in 1952.

John Anderson ran as an independent presidential candidate in 1980. Did he enter the 1984 race?

No. Anderson endorsed Walter Mondale in the 1984 election.

The Democrats claimed that they registered more than 5.5 million new voters in 1984. What was unusual about the voters they signed up at MacArthur Park in Los Angeles?

About 1,100 of these new voters lived in the park. A lawyer convinced the Los Angeles County registrar of voters that someone who sleeps on the same park bench or sidewalk grating every night has a regular "domicile" as defined in California election law.

On what grounds did Mondale attack the Reagan farm policies?

Mondale deplored the large number of farmers who had lost their farms due to mortgage foreclosures while Reagan was in the White House. He also assailed the Reagan administration for relying too heavily on its price support program that paid farmers not to grow crops. Describing American agricultural abundance as "a gift from God," Mondale called for stabilizing farm income by cutting the federal deficit, thereby reducing the value of the dollar overseas and making it easier for U.S. trading partners to increase purchases of American farm products.

How did the presidential candidates feel about the Equal Rights Amendment?

Mondale supported it, and Reagan opposed it.

How did the candidates differ on improving education?

Mondale said he would seek more federal funds to improve schools by attracting and keeping good teachers, modernizing laboratories, and strengthening graduate studies. He favored more college loans for the less affluent students and wanted more government support for the education of minorities and needy children. Reagan believed that state governments should take the lead in promoting educational reforms and that federal funds should be reserved primarily for the disadvantaged and handicapped.

Mondale opposed and Reagan favored tuition tax credits to parents of private-school pupils. Reagan supported merit pay for superior teachers, but Mondale did not endorse merit pay, which is a controversial issue in teacher organizations.

Why were pocketbook issues probably the most important plus factor in Reagan's reelection campaign?

Although the country had suffered a severe recession in 1981 and 1982, millions of Americans gave the President some of the credit for the improvement in their own economic positions in 1983 and 1984. Inflation had dropped dramatically since

Reagan took office, and interest rates were lower than when Jimmy Carter left the White House. Many people paid smaller taxes to the federal government and had greater purchasing power. Numerous industries were expanding and providing many new jobs.

Did the economic recovery under Reagan benefit most Americans about equally?

No. The overall unemployment rate in 1984 was about the same as it had been in 1981, and people on the lower rungs of the economic ladder generally did not share the prosperity of the more affluent citizens. While the top one-fifth of all households saw their purchasing power after taxes rise 9 percent during the Reagan administration, the bottom one-fifth of all families—those with incomes below $12,000 a year—saw their buying power drop by 8 percent. The Census Bureau reported that the number of Americans living in poverty totaled 35.3 million in 1983, an increase of more than 9 million since 1979. Black families suffered the worst economic decline. The median income of black families was $818 lower in 1983 than in 1980, after adjusting the figures for inflation, and the rate of unemployment for blacks was about double the rate for whites.

Why did Representative Patricia Schroeder describe Reagan as the "Teflon President"?

Because, she said, nothing bad seemed to stick to the President.

Reagan promised to "rearm America" when he ran for the presidency in 1980. To what extent was this promise kept?

President Reagan presided over the largest peacetime military buildup in United States history. Annual defense spending increases, when adjusted for inflation, averaged about 10 percent between 1981 and 1984. The Reagan administration's "strategic modernization" program included such major defense items as the 10-warhead MX intercontinental ballistic missile (ICBM), the single-warhead mobile ICBM called the "midgetman," the B-1 bomber, and submarines with nuclear missiles. Also, over the next five years the administration planned to spend about $25 billion on space-based antimissile defenses (dubbed "Star Wars" by opponents).

What national defense program did Mondale advocate?

Promising a military defense that would be "smart, lean, and tough," Mondale said that if elected President he would install a Pentagon budget that would increase by 3 or 4 percent a year but would total $25 billion less than the Reagan administration projected through 1989. Mondale would drop the MX missile, the B-1 bomber, and plans for space-based missile defenses. He would support ground-based and air-launched cruise missiles, the "stealth" bomber, new Trident submarine-launched nuclear missiles, and the ICBM "midgetman."

What were the two major differences between Mondale and Reagan in regard to dealing with the Soviet Union?

Mondale advocated a mutually verifiable nuclear weapons freeze. Reagan opposed such a freeze but offered tradeoffs in the reduction of key weapons as a first step in slowing the arms race. Mondale committed himself to a U.S.-Soviet summit meeting within six months of taking office and to subsequent annual meetings. Reagan proposed a step-by-step approach to summitry with Cabinet-level meetings preparing the way, which, he said, would enhance the possibility that a summit meeting would be productive.

What issue in Central America provoked the sharpest disagreement between Reagan and Mondale?

The issue of helping the CIA-supported Nicaraguan rebels to keep attacking the left-wing Sandinistas that are supported by Communist countries. Praising these *contra* rebels as freedom fighters, Reagan wanted the United States to continue sending them aid. Mondale argued that the United States should not be involved in covert actions to help the rebels. Also, he criticized our mining Nicaraguan harbors and the publication of a CIA manual that he said endorsed the assassination of Sandinista leaders.

What major issues were discussed in the first televised debate between Mondale and Reagan on October 7?

Domestic issues, including taxation, the budget and trade deficits, Social Security, abortion, school prayer, and the role of religion in politics.

In the eyes of the public who "won" this debate?

Most polls showed that the public was more favorably impressed by Mondale's performance, both in style and in the substance of his arguments. Mondale was perceived as poised and confident, aggressive and yet respectful, and well informed about the issues. Reagan was viewed as uncharacteristically ill at ease, hesitant and rambling in some of his remarks, and perhaps tiring in the last half-hour of the 90-minute debate.

How did each political camp react to this first debate?

Before the debate Mondale was trailing Reagan badly in all the polls, with some showing him more than 20 points behind and losing in nearly every state. So Democrats hailed Mondale's strong showing in the first debate as providing a new momentum for his sagging campaign. They felt it also raised a new election issue—Reagan's age (73) and his mental alertness to cope with problems in the Oval Office.

Republican leaders were not delighted with Reagan's below-par performance, but they maintained that Mondale had not delivered a "knockout blow," which they said was necessary if the Democratic challenger had any chance to hurt the President's quest for a second term.

Was the gender gap evident in the public's reaction to the one TV debate between the vice-presidential candidates?

Yes. An ABC News poll taken an hour after the debate on October 11 between George Bush and Geraldine Ferraro showed that Bush was the choice of 46 percent of the male viewers to 29 percent for Ferraro, but women viewers gave the edge to Ferraro, 38 percent to 37 percent. In a Gannett Poll Bush was seen as the winner by 59 percent of the men to 18 percent for Ferraro, with 19 percent calling it a tie. Among women, however, it was almost even—39 percent for Bush, 38 percent for Ferraro, with 16 percent viewing it as a tie.

Reagan and Mondale had a second and final debate on October 21. Which candidate was judged to have "won" this debate?

The second debate, which dealt with national defense and foreign policy, was considered much closer than the first encounter, and most polls gave the victory to Reagan. Probably the most important effect of this debate was that Reagan's strong performance reduced concerns about his age and convinced many TV viewers that the President still was a vigorous leader and the "Great Communicator."

How did the Reagan-Mondale debates affect the candidates' standings in the polls?

Following the first debate Mondale narrowed Reagan's lead in most polls by a few percentage points, but after the second debate Reagan regained his huge lead, which continued to increase during the last two weeks of the campaign.

On the day before the election did any major poll show that Mondale was in striking distance of overtaking Reagan?

No. Reagan led in the Gallup Poll by 18 points (which was the actual margin by which he won the election). Other major polls showed the President leading by 10 to 25 points.

On November 6, 1984, Ronald Reagan won a spectacular victory that stretched from coast to coast. How many states were in his victory column?

Reagan carried 49 states, losing to Mondale only Minnesota and the District of Columbia.

How many electoral votes did each candidate win?

Reagan won 525 electoral votes and Mondale won only 13.

Was the gender gap evident, as expected, in the election results?

Yes, but the Republican ticket still carried the vote of both sexes. Men voted 62 percent for Reagan and Bush and 38 percent for Mondale and Ferraro, while women chose the GOP candidates over the Democratic ticket by 54 percent to 46 percent.

How large was the margin that white voters gave to the Republican ticket?

Reagan and Bush won the white vote by an astounding 63 percent to 37 percent.

Jimmy Carter in 1980 also won less than half of the white vote. How long has it been since the Democratic presidential

candidate won a majority of the white vote?

The last Democratic presidential candidate to win more than half of the white vote was Lyndon B. Johnson in 1964.

Did black voters support Mondale in overwhelming numbers?

Yes. Mondale won about 91 percent of the black vote nationwide and 86 percent of the vote in the heavily black District of Columbia.

Did Reagan attract a larger Hispanic vote in 1984 or 1980?

Reagan won 44 percent of the Hispanic vote in 1984 but only 37 percent in 1980.

By how large a margin did the Republican ticket capture the 1984 Protestant vote?

Even though the fathers of Walter Mondale and his wife both were Protestant ministers, the Republicans won the Protestant vote by a whopping 66 percent to 34 percent.

With Catholic Geraldine Ferraro on the ticket were the Democrats able to salvage the Catholic vote?

No. Reagan won about 56 percent of the Catholic vote.

Did Mondale carry the Jewish vote?

Yes. Mondale carried the Jewish vote by 69 percent to 31 percent, which was a few percentage points higher than Carter's Jewish vote in 1980.

Did the vote of independents split more than three-to-two in favor of the Republican ticket?

Yes.

Did Mondale win the vote of people in the lowest income groups?

Yes. Mondale won the majority of families earning less than $10,000 a year, but Reagan carried all the groups with an annual income of $10,000 or more.

Did Reagan make deep inroads into the union vote?

Yes. Despite the strong support from the AFL-CIO and teacher groups, Mondale won the union vote by only about 55 percent to 45 percent.

Did any region of the country vote more strongly for Reagan than other regions?

Yes. Reagan carried the South with 62 percent of the vote, the West with 60 percent, the Midwest with 58 percent, and even the Northeast with 55 percent.

Was Reagan victorious among all age groups?

Yes. He swept every age group by a margin of about three-to-two, but his lead in the age group under 30 was smaller than some polls had predicted.

How near did Reagan come to making the election a 50-states sweep?

Reagan lost Minnesota by about 15,000 votes out of more than 2 million votes cast.

In 1980 Utah provided Reagan's largest winning margin over Carter. Did this happen again in 1984?

Yes, but in 1984 Reagan carried about 75 percent of the vote compared with 72 percent in 1980.

What three other states did Reagan win with 70 percent or more of the vote?

Idaho, Nebraska, and Wyoming.

Reagan carried what other six states by a margin of more than two-to-one?

Alaska, Arizona, Kansas, Nevada, New Hampshire, and Oklahoma.

Reagan won what state that never before had been captured by a Republican, except by Richard Nixon in 1972?

Hawaii.

What three other states that voted Democratic in five of the last six presidential elections were also carried by Reagan?

Maryland, Massachusetts, and Rhode Island. However, these three states gave Reagan his narrowest victory margins. He carried Massachusetts with about 51 percent of the vote and Rhode Island and Maryland with 52 percent.

How close did the Democrats come to winning Geraldine Ferraro's home state of New York?

The Democrats lost New York by 46 percent to 54 percent.

Did Ronald Reagan and George Bush win their home states by gigantic margins?

Yes. They carried California by 58 percent to 42 percent and Texas by 64 percent to 36 percent.

Did the Democrats have anything to cheer about in the 1984 elections?

Yes, the Reagan landslide did not spill over to the gubernatorial and congressional elections, which led some analysts to conclude that Reagan's huge victory was mainly a personal triumph for a very popular President rather than an indication that the GOP had emerged as the nation's dominant political party.

In 13 gubernatorial races the Republicans won only one additional statehouse. They elected four new governors in North Carolina, Rhode Island, Utah, and West Virginia, but the GOP lost its governors' seats in North Dakota, Washington, and Vermont. Republicans also fell short of their goals in congressional races. (See pages 193–194.)

What factors accounted for Reagan's enormous personal victory at the polls?

It is very difficult to unseat any incumbent President during a period of relative peace and prosperity. Reagan won a second term in the White House partly because of the solid accomplishments of his first term—lower taxes, lower inflation, lower interest rates, more purchasing power; greater national pride and a resurgent dedication to spiritual and family values; an increased national defense and the refusal to be intimidated by the Soviets. Moreover, the huge size of the President's vote obviously was enhanced by his personal qualities. Many voters perceived Reagan as a strong, effective leader, as the most charismatic and ennobling communicator in the White House since John F. Kennedy, as a President committed to championing personal initiative and to ending government expenditures to those who are not truly needy, and as a persistent prophet of optimism who envisions a bright future for Americans in their quest for a "shining city on a hill."

Reagan's decisive win was due in part also to the Democrats' flaws and failures. The intense intraparty rivalry among Walter Mondale, Gary Hart, and Jesse Jackson left deep wounds that were hard to heal; Mondale was accused of being the puppet of special interest groups, especially labor unions; the financial problems of Geraldine Ferraro hurt the Democrats' cause, and Mondale's candid demand for higher taxes was unpopular with many voters. Also, Mondale failed to articulate any issues that caught fire with the public, and he was burdened by his close association with the largely unsuccessful Carter administration.

How many times in the history of our two major political parties has a Vice-President who was defeated for reelection (which happened to Mondale in 1980) been his party's presidential nominee four years later?

This has never occurred before.

Some experts predicted that over 100 million voters would troop to the polls in 1984. Did this happen?

No. The total vote in 1984 was about 92 million, which was an increase of about 5.5 million over the vote in 1980. Still, about 47 percent of the total adult population did not vote. This means that nearly half of all eligible Americans squandered the most precious right that people who live in a democracy have.

* * * * *

The next four chapters discuss the results of the presidential elections since 1856, when the rivalry between the Democratic and Republican parties began.

LANDSLIDE VICTORIES

*The only thing better than a close victory at the
polls is to win by a landslide. . .*

**The Democrats won their largest victory over the Republicans
in what presidential election?**

The Democrats annihilated the Republicans in 1964 when
President Lyndon B. Johnson was reelected by an unparalleled
vote margin over Senator Barry Goldwater. Millions of independent voters and moderate Republicans, as well as most
Democrats, regarded Goldwater as a conservative extremist.
Moreover, the 1964 election occurred before the escalation of
the Vietnam War, and President Johnson was at the peak of
his popularity.

Besides his native Arizona, Goldwater carried only five states,
all in the Deep South. Lyndon B. Johnson's 61.05 percent of
the popular vote was the highest percentage ever attained by a
Democratic presidential nominee (except when James Monroe
had no organized opposition in 1816 and 1820). Johnson's vote
total even surpassed the previous record set by Franklin D.
Roosevelt in the 1936 election.

1964 Election	% of popular vote	Electoral votes
Lyndon B. Johnson (D)	61.05	486
Barry Goldwater (R)	38.47	52

Did the Republicans ever come close to defeating Franklin D. Roosevelt in his four presidential elections?

No. In not one of FDR's four races did the Republicans win even one-fourth of the electoral votes. When Roosevelt ran for his fourth term in 1944, the Republicans made their strongest showing, but FDR still won handily in both popular votes and electoral votes.

The Roosevelt years were thoroughly frustrating to the GOP. In 1932 the Republicans nominated an incumbent President with a record of impeccable integrity (Herbert Hoover). Four years later their standard-bearer was a moderately conservative Kansas governor (Alfred M. Landon). In 1940 the Republicans selected an ex-Democrat, a homespun Hoosier with a rumpled appearance and a raspy voice (Wendell Willkie). And in 1944 they turned to the Eastern Establishment for a progressive New York governor with a proven record as a spectacular vote-getter in what was then the nation's largest state (Thomas E. Dewey). But no matter what type of candidate was chosen, or which section of the country he came from, the Republicans were all losers to the unbeatable FDR.

The Roosevelt Reign

1932 Election	% of popular vote	Electoral votes
Franklin D. Roosevelt (D)	57.42	472
Herbert Hoover (R)	39.64	59

1936 Election	% of popular vote	Electoral votes
Franklin D. Roosevelt (D)	60.79	523
Alfred M. Landon (R)	36.54	8

1940 Election	% of popular vote	Electoral votes
Franklin D. Roosevelt (D)	54.70	449
Wendell Willkie (R)	44.82	82

1944 Election	% of popular vote	Electoral votes
Franklin D. Roosevelt (D)	53.39	432
Thomas E. Dewey (R)	45.89	99

Once a Democratic presidential candidate won an election in which the Republican nominee finished in third place. When did this happen?

In 1912 when two Republican Presidents ran against each other, and a former professor beat them both! Former President Theodore Roosevelt, disappointed in the White House performance of his successor, William Howard Taft, wanted the job back for himself. When the GOP convention renominated President Taft, Roosevelt accepted the third-party nomination of the Progressive "Bull Moose" Party.

The Democrats nominated for the presidency Governor Woodrow Wilson of New Jersey. Taking advantage of the severe rift in the Republican Party, Wilson won the electoral vote by landslide proportions. He carried all except eight states, and his electoral-vote total was more than four times the combined total of Roosevelt and Taft.

Roosevelt captured six states and 88 electoral votes. But Republican nominee Taft finished a distant third, carrying only two states—Utah and Vermont, with a total of 8 electoral votes. He didn't even win New Hampshire, which had gone Republican in every presidential election since the GOP was born.

Since Roosevelt and Taft together outpolled Wilson by over 1,300,000 votes, the former Rough Rider might have defeated Wilson in a two-man race. But this isn't a certainty, because the Democratic Party was in the midst of a growth spurt and in 1910 had gained control of the House of Representatives for the first time since 1892. To futher complicate the 1912 election, a fourth-party candidate, Socialist Eugene V. Debs, polled over 900,000 votes.

1912 Election	% of popular vote	Electoral votes
Woodrow Wilson (D)	41.84	435
Theodore Roosevelt (P)	27.39	88
William Howard Taft (R)	23.18	8
Eugene V. Debs (S)	5.99	0

CLIFF-HANGERS

A win is a win, no matter whether it is
by a landslide or a whisker.

In what presidential election since World War II did the Democratic nominee win the popular vote by only .17 percent?

In 1960, when Senator John F. Kennedy of Massachusetts defeated Vice-President Richard Nixon by this razor-thin margin. A record-breaking 68,828,960 Americans trooped to the polls, and the final tally showed Kennedy winning by 114,673 votes.

1960 Election	% of popular vote	Electoral votes
John F. Kennedy (D)	49.72	303
Richard Nixon (R)	49.55	219
Harry F. Byrd (D) *	0	15

*All of Mississippi's eight electors, together with six electors from Alabama and one from Oklahoma, cast their ballots for noncandidate Harry F. Byrd, a conservative Democratic senator from Virginia.

Kennedy carried three large states—Illinois, New Jersey, and Missouri—and several smaller states by less than 1 percent of the popular vote. His margin in Illinois was less than 9,000 votes out of nearly 4,750,000; in Hawaii Kennedy won by 115 votes out of about 450,000. Only a small shift of votes in some of these very close states would have given the election to Nixon.

Did the Democratic nominee in any other presidential election win by less than 1 percent of the popular vote?

Yes. In 1884 only .25 percent of the popular vote separated the triumphant Democrat from the defeated Republican. The winner was Governor Grover Cleveland of New York; the loser was former House Speaker James G. Blaine.

The race for electoral votes was very close, too, with New York playing the key role of the make-or-break state. Cleveland carried New York, but if Blaine had taken that state, he would have had enough electoral votes to become the next President. More than 1,125,000 New Yorkers voted, and Cleveland's winning margin was 1,047!

1884 Election	% of popular vote	Electoral votes
Grover Cleveland (D)	48.50	219
James G. Blaine (R)	48.25	182

What part did the phrase "Rum, Romanism, and Rebellion" play in the outcome of this close 1884 election?

Shortly before the election, Blaine met with a group of sympathetic Protestant ministers. One of the clergymen told Blaine, "We are Republicans and don't propose to leave our party and identify ourselves with the party whose antecedents have been rum, Romanism, and rebellion."

The newspapers widely publicized the phrase "Rum, Romanism, and Rebellion," which was a vicious insult to the many Roman Catholics and Southerners in the Democratic Party. This ugly slur undoubtedly caused some Catholics in the close Northern states to switch their votes from Blaine to Cleveland. Indeed, it may have been the factor that clinched New York for Cleveland and assured him of becoming the first Democratic President since the Civil War.

How did a third-party candidate help Cleveland return to the White House?

In 1888 Cleveland was defeated for reelection by Benjamin Harrison, but four years later the situation was reversed, and Cleveland ousted Harrison from the White House. Cleveland's successful comeback in 1892 was partly due to the strong campaign waged by James B. Weaver, the Populist Party candidate, in Western mining states and Midwestern farm states.

Weaver drew most of his support from people who generally voted Republican. He captured three states—Colorado, Kansas, and Nevada—that had been in the Republican column in 1888, and he also won the new state of Idaho that was participating in its first presidential election. In five other states that the Democrats won, the combined vote total for Harrison and Weaver was larger than Cleveland's winning margin.

California was one of the five states in which Weaver's candidacy helped Cleveland. There couldn't be a much closer race than the one the Golden State provided in 1892.

California results	Votes	%
Grover Cleveland	118,151	43.8
Benjamin Harrison	118,027	43.8
James B. Weaver	25,311	9.4

1892 Election	% of popular vote	Electoral votes
Benjamin Harrison (R)	42.96	145
Grover Cleveland (D)	46.05	277
James B. Weaver (P)	8.50	22

What election in this century was so close that the winner was not determined until the last state reported its results?

In the 1916 election President Woodrow Wilson ran for a second term against Republican Charles Evans Hughes, a Supreme Court justice. The early returns indicated that Hughes was the apparent winner. He had carried all the big Eastern states and most of the Midwest. All that Hughes still needed to win was California, and this Western state had not been taken by the Democrats in 24 years. So Hughes's personal staff had started addressing their boss as "Mr. President-elect."

On Thursday afternoon, two days after the election, Hughes took a nap and gave his secretary orders not to disturb him.

While he was napping, a reporter phoned and asked to speak to Hughes.

"I'm sorry," Hughes's secretary replied, "but the President-elect is sleeping and cannot be disturbed."

"All right," grumbled the reporter, "but when Hughes wakes up tell him that he isn't the President-elect." The final returns from California had just come in, and Wilson had carried the state by about 3,400 votes out of more than 928,000 votes that were cast.

If Hughes had captured California's 13 electoral votes, he would have gone to the White House with 1 more electoral vote than the required majority.

1916 Election	% of popular vote	Electoral votes
Woodrow Wilson (D)	49.24	277
Charles Evans Hughes (R)	46.11	254

What small snub in California may have cost Hughes the presidency?

At the same time that Hughes was running for President, Governor Hiram Johnson of California (who belonged to the progressive wing of the Republican Party) was seeking a Senate seat. One day when Hughes was campaigning in Long Beach, California, Johnson was staying at the same hotel. Political etiquette dictated that Hughes should pay a courtesy call on the California governor, but such a meeting was never arranged, and Johnson angrily concluded that Hughes had snubbed him.

So Johnson refused to campaign actively for Hughes in California. On election day Johnson won his Senate seat by a huge margin of 300,000 votes, but when Republicans looked for his coattails Hughes was nowhere to be found.

Why did the 1948 presidential election provide the most startling upset in our political history?

Harry Truman was running for the Democrats, and the Republicans felt supremely confident in 1948 that they would regain the presidency for the first time in 20 years. The Democratic administration was besmirched by charges of corruption and accused of being soft on Communism. Moreover, Truman lacked the charismatic appeal of his predecessor in the White House, Franklin D. Roosevelt. Polls gave the Truman administration very low marks and indicated that many Americans felt that the feisty little man with steel-rimmed glasses and a nasal Missouri twang was not qualified to continue as President.

Then, too, in 1948 the Democratic Party was in dreadful disarray and split into three warring factions. Truman occupied the middle ground in the party. To his left were those Democrats who felt the administration had been too tough on the Communists, and they ran former Vice-President Henry Wallace as their presidential candidate. To Truman's right were many Southern segregationists, who were unhappy with the party platform's strong stand on civil rights. They bolted the Democratic convention, formed the new States' Rights "Dixiecrat" Party, and chose South Carolina Governor J. Strom Thurmond to be their presidential nominee.

The Republicans selected for their ticket an attractive pair of moderate governors from two large states—New Yorker Thomas E. Dewey for President and Earl Warren of California for Vice-President.

Pollsters were so certain that Dewey would win the election by a landslide that they quit sampling voters' opinions in mid-October. But the surprising election results gave the Republicans apoplexy and Truman another term in the White House.

1948 Election	% of popular vote	Electoral votes
Harry S Truman (D)	49.51	303
Thomas E Dewey (R)	45.12	189
J. Strom Thurmond (SR)	2.40	39
Henry Wallace (P)	2.38	0

Why did Truman score this astonishing triumph?

There were various reasons for Truman's upset victory, but three stand out as particularly important. (1) The desertion from the Democratic ranks of the Wallace left-wingers and the Thurmond right-wingers may actually have helped Truman because he could then be perceived as a moderate, and most voters consider themselves moderates rather than extremists. (2) The Republicans were vastly overconfident, and Dewey's campaign was too placid to excite the voters and turn the election into an all-out GOP crusade. (3) President Truman pled his case convincingly in the heartland of America. Launching an effective "whistle-stop" campaign, he spoke from the train's rear platform in plain but forceful words that praised the Democrats' accomplishments and scorned the Republican-dominated 80th Congress as a "do-nothing" legislature.

If Truman had lost two states that he carried by very narrow margins, the 1948 election would have been the first decided in the House of Representatives since 1825. What two states were they?

California and Ohio, each with 25 electoral votes. If Dewey had won these states, Truman's electoral-vote total would have been cut to 253, or 13 votes short of the 266 needed to win a majority. The figures below show how close the nation came to having the President selected by the House of Representatives.

State	Truman	Dewey	Margin of Truman's Plurality
California	1,913,134	1,895,269	17,865
Ohio	1,452,791	1,445,684	7,107

How small was Jimmy Carter's margin of victory in 1976?

On the eve of the 1976 election most pollsters said the contest was too close to call, and the election results proved this forecast was correct. Carter had a bare 50.1 percent of the popular vote and only 27 more electoral votes than the 270 needed to win.

1976 Election	% of popular vote	Electoral votes
Jimmy Carter (D)	50.1	297
Gerald Ford (R)	48.0	240
Eugene McCarthy (I)*	0.9	0
Ronald Reagan **	0	1

*Former Senator Eugene McCarthy of Minnesota ran as an Independent candidate.
**A Ford elector from the state of Washington broke ranks and cast his electoral vote for noncandidate Ronald Reagan.

Carter captured four states by just a whisker. If Ford had taken Ohio (which he lost by about 11,000 votes out of more than four million cast) and any one of these three other states, he would have been returned to the White House for another term:

State	Electoral votes	Carter	Ford	McCarthy
Hawaii	4	147,375	140,003	0
Mississippi	7	381,309	366,846	4,074
Ohio	25	2,011,621	2,000,505	58,258
Wisconsin	11	1,040,232	1,004,987	34,943

What court ruling during the 1976 campaign may have cost Ford the election?

A court in New York ruled against permitting Independent Eugene McCarthy's name on the ballot in that state. McCarthy, the former antiwar senator from Minnesota, had a large liberal following in New York, and most of these liberals probably voted for Carter rather than Ford. Since Carter carried New York by less than 300,000 votes out of about 6,500,000, some political analysts believe that if McCarthy had been a candidate there, he would have taken enough votes away from Carter to give New York and the election to Ford.

Did McCarthy's candidacy make any significant difference in the election results in other states?

Eugene McCarthy polled less than 1 percent of the popular vote, but if he had not been in the race it is likely that Carter's victory would have been larger. In four states (with a total of 26 electoral votes) that were won by Ford, the combined Carter-McCarthy vote total was larger than Ford's. These four states were Iowa, Maine, Oklahoma, and Oregon.

In 1856, the first election in which the new Republican Party ran a presidential candidate, Democrat James Buchanan won the electoral vote by a comfortable margin. Did Buchanan also win a majority of the popular vote?

No. In 1856 Buchanan faced two major rivals, Republican

John Charles Frémont and former President Millard Fillmore who ran on the "Know-Nothing" ticket. Buchanan polled 1,836,072 votes, but the combined vote total of Frémont and Fillmore was 2,215,398.

1856 Election	% of popular vote	Electoral votes
James Buchanan (D)	45.28	174
John Charles Frémont (R)	33.11	114
Millard Fillmore (KN)	21.53	8

NEAR MISSES

As every Monday morning quarterback knows, a narrow defeat prompts the plaintive refrain, "Damn it, if only we had. . ."

Since 1960, has any Democratic candidate lost a presidential election by less than 1 percent of the popular vote?

Yes. Hubert Humphrey lost the 1968 election to Richard Nixon by a popular-vote margin of only .7 percent. The 1968 election presented a double-barreled problem to Humphrey. Besides contesting against Nixon, Humphrey had to contend with the strong third-party candidacy of George Wallace, the former governor of Alabama, who was the nominee of the American Independent Party. Wallace captured five Southern states and 46 electoral votes. Moreover, he amassed nearly ten million popular votes, setting a new record for third-party candidates.

1968 Election	% of popular vote	Electoral votes
Richard Nixon (R)	43.42	301
Hubert Humphrey (D)	42.72	191
George Wallace (AI)	13.53	46

Although Nixon defeated Humphrey by 110 electoral votes, how might small voting shifts in a few states have brought victory to the Democrat?

The results in a few states shown below suggest several ways that Humphrey might have triumphed in the electoral vote. While Nixon carried all of these states, notice that in each of them the combined votes for Humphrey and Wallace exceeded the number of votes for Nixon.

State	Electoral votes	Nixon	Humphrey	Wallace
California	40	3,467,664	3,244,318	487,270
Florida	14	886,804	676,794	624,207
Illinois	26	2,174,774	2,039,814	390,958
Missouri	12	811,932	791,444	206,126
New Jersey	17	1,325,467	1,264,206	262,187
Ohio	26	1,791,014	1,700,586	467,495
Wisconsin	12	809,997	748,804	127,835

If Humphrey had taken just 32 more electoral votes from Nixon, the election would have gone to the House of Representatives, which was controlled by the Democrats and almost certainly would have elected Humphrey. This could have happened if the Democrats had added to their win column the single state of California or any combination of states with an electoral-vote total of at least 32. Humphrey could have won the election outright if he had picked up 79 of Nixon's electoral votes. Had Nixon lost to Humphrey about 112,000 votes in California, about 68,000 votes in Illinois, and about 46,000 votes in Ohio, Humphrey would have won the election in a breeze—with 283 electoral votes to Nixon's 209. This change would have involved only about a quarter-million votes out of the 73 million that were cast!

In what nineteenth-century presidential election did the Democratic candidate lose by a popular-vote margin of only .02 percent?

In the 1880 election Democrat Winfield S. Hancock lost to Republican James A. Garfield by the narrowest popular-vote margin in history. A total of 9,210,420 votes were cast, and Garfield's plurality was only 1,898 votes! The GOP nominee had a much wider lead in the electoral vote because he captured six of the seven most heavily populated states.

Third-party candidate James B. Weaver of the Greenback Party polled over 300,000 votes. But Weaver carried no states, and the votes cast for him did not affect the outcome in any state, except possibly California, which Hancock captured by 144 votes out of more than 164,000 ballots cast.

1880 Election	% of popular vote	Electoral votes
James A. Garfield (R)	48.27	214
Winfield S. Hancock (D)	48.25	155
James B. Weaver (G)	3.32	0

In what presidential campaign did the Democratic nominee lose by a single electoral vote?

This was the famous "disputed" election of 1876 in which Republican Rutherford B. Hayes, governor of Ohio, defeated Democrat Samuel J. Tilden, governor of New York. On election day it appeared that Tilden had won. He led his GOP opponent by a quarter-million popular votes and captured 184 of the 185 electoral votes needed for victory. Hayes had only 166 electoral votes, 19 short of the magic number.

These 19 electoral votes, from the states of Florida, Louisiana, and South Carolina, were disputed. Each party vigorously claimed that its candidate had won all three of these Southern states. Tempers flared and tension mounted as the Democrats and Republicans angrily charged each other with attempted bribes, voter intimidation, stuffed and stolen ballot boxes, and falsified election returns.

Congress was compelled to take some action, and finally it established a special 15-member electoral commission to investigate the disputes and decide how the electoral votes in each of the three states should be counted. The electoral commission included five congressmen, five senators, and five Supreme Court justices. Eight members of the commission were Republicans; seven were Democrats. Even so, the Democratic Party leaders felt that the commission surely would decide that Tilden had won the election, since all that he needed to reach the White House was one more electoral vote.

But on each of the disputes the commission voted along straight party lines, and by an 8-7 margin gave Hayes all of the

19 electoral votes, thus withholding from Tilden the 1 precious vote that would have made him the first Democratic President since before the Civil War.

1876 Election	% of popular vote	Electoral votes
Rutherford B. Hayes (R)	47.95	185
Samuel J. Tilden (D)	50.97	184

In this 1876 election one man really decided who would be the next President. Who was he?

When Congress .appointed the original electoral commission, it consisted of seven Republicans and seven Democrats. The 15th member was Justice David Davis, who was considered a political independent. Leaders of both parties felt that Davis would be unbiased and fair in reaching his decision on the disputed votes. But an unforeseen development occurred when the Illinois legislature named Davis to a seat in the Senate. Davis then resigned from the electoral commission, and his place was taken by Justice Joseph P. Bradley. Although Bradley was a Republican, the Democrats felt he would be less biased than any of the remaining justices, all of whom were also Republicans.

A delegation of Democratic leaders called on Bradley the night before the electoral commission was to vote on the disputes, and they came away from the meeting confident that Bradley's key vote would make Tilden the next President.

But the following morning Justice Joseph P. Bradley cast the decisive vote that sent Hayes to the Executive Mansion.

The 1876 election nearly left the United States without a President. How did this happen?

Angry Democrats throughout the nation raised a mighty storm of protest, charging that Tilden had been robbed of the presidency. In some areas they began gathering arms, forming volunteer companies, and threatening to start a second civil war if Hayes went to the White House.

Meanwhile the Democratic-controlled House of Representatives refused to accept the verdict of the electoral commission. It planned to filibuster, so that the official electoral count could not be completed before inauguration day, March 4. If this happened, the United States would be without a President after the term of the outgoing Chief Executive expired the same day.

The haunting prospect of a leaderless country increased with every passing day. Finally, as inauguration day neared, the leaders of both parties agreed to a compromise. The Democrats would end the congressional filibuster and accept Hayes as President, while the Republicans promised to remove the last federal troops from the South, thus ending Reconstruction.

On March 2, 1877, the presiding officer of the Senate announced that Hayes had been elected President. The new Chief Executive took his oath of office the following day because March 4 was a Sunday. The formal inauguration took place on March 5, and the crisis that could have led to another civil war was resolved.

Was there any other presidential election in which the Democrat had more popular votes than the Republican but still lost the election?

Yes, this happened again in 1888 when Republican Benjamin Harrison took the White House away from the incumbent Democrat, Grover Cleveland. Although Cleveland had a plurality of over 90,000 votes, he did not capture any of the four states with more than 20 electoral votes—New York (36), Pennsylvania (30), Ohio (23), and Illinois (22). Harrison also carried all of New England except Connecticut, most of the Midwestern states, and all of the states west of Missouri except Texas.

Since Harrison won all of the four largest states and many of the smaller ones, why didn't he have more popular votes than Cleveland?

Because Harrison won most of his states by *slim* margins, while Cleveland won nearly all the Southern states by *huge* margins. Cleveland carried South Carolina with 82 percent of the popular vote, Louisiana and Mississippi with 73 percent, Georgia with 70 percent, and Alabama with 67 percent. Since Cleveland won the smaller Southern states by lopsided amounts, this offset Harrison's narrow victories in many closely contested states and enabled Cleveland to win more popular votes than the man who defeated him.

1888 Election	% of popular vote	Electoral votes
Benjamin Harrison (R)	47.82	233
Grover Cleveland (D)	48.62	168

What endorsement of Cleveland in this close election proved to be the "kiss of death"?

A Harrison supporter in California posed as a former British citizen and wrote the British minister in Washington, asking how he should vote in the upcoming presidential election. The naive British diplomat fell into the trap set for him. He answered that Queen Victoria's government would be delighted to see President Cleveland reelected. When the jubilant Californian received this reply, he hastened to have it printed in the newspaper. Publicizing the letter had the effect that its sly recipient desired. Cleveland was called the "British candidate," which infuriated large numbers of Irish voters who hated anything British. In heavily Irish Massachusetts the Republican vote jumped from 48.4 percent in 1884 to 53.4 percent in 1888. Even more important was what happened in New York, with its large number of Irish-Americans. The state had given its 36 electoral votes to Cleveland in 1884, but when the "British question" surfaced in 1888, Harrison took New York from Cleveland. So in this very close election the Irish vote may have tipped the scales to Harrison, even though, ironically, Cleveland himself was part Irish.

DEBACLES

Today's tragedy may be the beginning of tomorrow's triumph—
but tomorrow won't come for another four years.

In 1984 Walter Mondale won only 13 electoral votes, one state, and the District of Columbia. How did his loss to Ronald Reagan compare with Jimmy Carter's loss in 1980?
Carter won 49 electoral votes, six states, and the District of Columbia.

What other Democratic presidential candidate in this century also won only a single state?
Senator George McGovern of South Dakota, who lost the 1972 election to President Richard Nixon. McGovern carried just one state, Massachusetts, and the District of Columbia.

1972 Election	% of popular vote	Electoral votes
Richard Nixon (R)	60.69	520
George McGovern (D)	37.53	17

Of all the candidates since George Washington, who won the most popular votes in a presidential election?
Ronald Reagan, who won about 53.5 million votes in 1984.

Another Democratic debacle occurred when joining the League of Nations was a major issue with the American voters. Who were the candidates in that election?

Republican Senator Warren G. Harding of Ohio, who defeated Democratic Governor James M. Cox, also of Ohio, in 1920.

1920 Election	% of popular vote	Electoral votes
Warren G. Harding (R)	60.30	404
James M. Cox (D)	34.17	127

The Democrats suffered another stinging defeat during a boom period when voters continued to support the "party of prosperity." What Catholic Democratic candidate lost that election?

Governor Alfred E. Smith of New York, who was trounced by Secretary of Commerce Herbert Hoover in 1928.

1928 Election	% of popular vote	Electoral votes
Herbert Hoover (R)	58.20	444
Alfred E. Smith (D)	40.77	87

Who was the only Democratic presidential nominee to lose twice to the same opponent in the twentieth century?

Governor Adlai E. Stevenson of Illinois, who was beaten by the World War II hero Dwight D. Eisenhower in 1952 and 1956. Notice that in the rematch between these two candidates Stevenson lost by a larger margin than he did in their first encounter.

1952 Election	% of popular vote	Electoral votes
Dwight D. Eisenhower (R)	55.13	442
Adlai E. Stevenson (D)	44.38	89

1956 Election	% of popular vote	Electoral votes
Dwight D. Eisenhower (R)	57.37	457
Adlai E. Stevenson (D)	41.97	73

In the first decade of this century, what colorless New York judge was overwhelmed at the polls by a colorful President?

Democrat Alton B. Parker, who was badly beaten in 1904 by President Theodore Roosevelt in his bid for a full four-year term in the White House.

1904 Election	% of popular vote	Electoral votes
Theodore Roosevelt (R)	56.41	336
Alton B. Parker (D)	37.60	140

What other Republican President, in his race for reelection, triumphed easily over an opponent who ran both as a Democrat and as a Liberal Republican?

Ulysses S. Grant crushed publisher Horace Greeley at the polls in 1872, even though Greeley was the candidate of both the Democratic Party and the anti-Grant Liberal Republicans.

1872 Election	% of popular vote	Electoral votes
Ulysses S. Grant (R)	55.63	286
Horace Greeley (D.,LR)	43.83	0*

*Greeley died between the date when the voters cast their ballots in November and the time that the electors voted in December, so his electors split their votes among four non-candidates.

What Democratic general ran for the presidency against his former commander-in-chief and lost by a lopsided margin?

General George McClellan, who, in 1864, failed to prevent Abraham Lincoln from winning a second term as President.

1864 Election	% of popular vote	Electoral votes
Abraham Lincoln (R)	55.02	212
George McClellan (D)	44.96	21

When was the only time that a Republican presidential candidate faced a strong third-party opponent, as well as the Democratic challenger, and still won with more than 54 percent of the popular vote?

This was in 1924 when President Calvin Coolidge defeated

Democrat John W. Davis and the Progressive candidate, Robert M. La Follette, who polled nearly 5 million votes but carried only his home state, Wisconsin.

1924 Election	% of popular vote	Electoral votes
Calvin Coolidge (R)	54.04	382
John W. Davis (D)	28.84	136
Robert M. La Follette (P)	16.56	13

How is it possible for a candidate to win a landslide in the electoral vote without necessarily winning a landslide in the popular vote?

When one candidate wins nearly all of the large states (with their big blocs of electoral votes) by narrow margins, that candidate can acquire a huge number of electoral votes without necessarily having a proportionate share of the popular vote. A good example of this was the 1868 election, in which General Ulysses S. Grant had almost three times as many electoral votes as Democrat Horatio Seymour had, yet Grant won in the popular vote by only about 5 percent.

1868 Election	% of popular vote	Electoral votes
Ulysses S. Grant (R)	52.66	214
Horatio Seymour (D)	47.34	80

What candidate won a landslide victory in the electoral vote although his three opponents amassed more than 60 percent of the popular vote?

In the 1860 election Abraham Lincoln had 57 more electoral votes than the combined total of three opponents, but he won the election with less than 40 percent of the popular vote.

1860 Election	% of popular vote	Electoral votes
Abraham Lincoln (R)	39.82	180
Stephen A. Douglas (D)	29.46	12
John C. Breckinridge (SD)	18.09	72
John Bell (CU)	12.61	39

Three out of every five voters did not want Lincoln as their President, yet he was elected because he carried the large Eastern and Midwestern states, generally by thin margins. His longtime rival, Stephen A. Douglas, ran a strong second in the states that Lincoln won, but Douglas captured only one state, Missouri, which explains his small number of electoral votes.

The Southern Democrats, who split the Democratic vote by refusing to support Douglas, ran Vice-President John C. Breckinridge of Kentucky as a sectional candidate. Breckinridge won 11 Southern states with 72 electoral votes, but he finished a poor third in the popular-vote column.

The fourth candidate, John Bell, represented the Constitutional Union Party, whose chief goal was to keep the Union together and avert a war between the North and South. Bell ran strongest in the border states, where there were both Northern and Southern sympathizers. Bell carried three states—Kentucky, Tennessee, and Virginia.

Were there any states where Lincoln received no votes in the 1860 election?

Yes. Ironically, many American voters in 1860 could not cast ballots for the man who is generally regarded as the greatest of all our Presidents. This was because Lincoln's name was not on the ballot in the Southern states of Alabama, Arkansas, Florida, Georgia, Louisiana, Mississippi, North Carolina, Tennessee, and Texas. In South Carolina the voters were not allowed to cast ballots for *any* presidential candidate until 1868. Before that date South Carolina's presidential electors were selected by the state legislature, not by the people.

Colorful William Jennings Bryan was a thorn in the side of Republicans for many years. Was this three-time loser beaten by larger margins in the electoral vote or the popular vote?

In all three presidential elections Bryan was defeated more decisively in the electoral vote than the popular vote. While Bryan carried 22 states to William McKinley's 23 states in 1896, Bryan still lost that election by 95 electoral votes. This was because McKinley won all the heavily populated Eastern states and most of the large Midwestern states, while Bryan's victories were mainly in more sparsely populated Western and Southern states and a few Midwestern states.

Nevertheless, Bryan proved to be a formidable campaigner. The figures below show that he held his Republican opponent to less than 52 percent of the popular vote in all three of his unsuccessful bids for the presidency.

1896 Election	% of popular vote	Electoral votes
William McKinley (R)	51.01	271
William Jennings Bryan (D, P*)	46.73	176

1900 Election		
William McKinley (R)	51.67	292
William Jennings Bryan (D)	45.51	155

1908 Election		
William Howard Taft (R)	51.58	321
William Jennings Bryan (D)	43.05	162

*In the 1896 election Bryan was the candidate of both the Democratic and Populist parties.

PAST LEADERS
IN CONGRESS

Who was known as "Spitting Lion" and "Ragged Mat the Democrat"?

Congressman Matthew Lyon of Vermont, who in 1798 spat a stream of tobacco juice in the face of Federalist Congressman Roger Griswold of Connecticut. When, after weeks of debate, the House failed to pass an official reprimand against Lyon, Griswold attacked him on the House floor with a hickory cane. Lyon seized fire tongs to fight back, and the two continued their conflict by wrestling on the floor.

Why was Matthew Lyon the first congressman to be jailed?

Lyon was sentenced to four months in jail when he violated the Sedition Act by publishing the opinion that President John Adams ought to be sent to an insane asylum. While he was in jail Democratic-Republican Lyon was reelected to the House. After his release, when Lyon set off for Congress, he was followed on the first day of his journey by a parade of admirers' carriages said to have been 12 miles long.

What cantankerous Virginian brought his dogs onto the floor of Congress, engaged in brawls with his colleagues, and fought a harmless duel with Henry Clay in 1826?

John Randolph, who served five terms in the House and two years in the Senate.

Who served a few months in the Senate while he was under 30, in violation of the Constitution?

Henry Clay, who had been elected to fill a vacancy in 1806. After his Senate term ended, he returned to the Kentucky House of Representatives, but in 1810 he was again elected to the Senate as a Democratic-Republican. Later Clay broke with his party and became a prominent Whig.

"Let us conquer space" was the bold cry of what early congressman, arguing for what legislation?

John C. Calhoun in 1817 used these words in advocating a federally subsidized network of roads and canals.

What new slang words were added to the American language by the long, irrelevant, rambling speeches of Congressman Felix Walker?

"Buncombe" (for "bunkum") and "bunk." Walker represented Buncombe County, North Carolina, in the House from 1817 to 1823. His lengthy, pointless speeches about Buncombe led his colleagues to change the name of that county into a derogatory word, and sometimes they shortened it to "bunk."

Who was the first man to serve in the Senate for 30 consecutive years?

Thomas Hart Benton of Missouri, who was a senator from 1821 to 1851.

What famous frontiersman, who claimed he had killed 105 bears, was elected to Congress first as a Democrat and later as a Whig?

David "Davy" Crockett served as a Tennessee Democratic congressman from 1827 to 1831, then switched to the Whigs, who elected him to another term, 1833-35.

Who was the chief spokesman for the South in the Senate from 1832 until his death in 1850?

John C. Calhoun of South Carolina, who strongly believed in states' rights, including the right to nullify federal laws.

The first president of the Texas Republic later became one of the first United States senators from Texas. Who was he?

Sam Houston, who wore a sombrero and a panther-fur vest

on the floor of Congress and sat at his desk whittling wood sticks. Although he supported the South's cause on some issues, Houston was a firm believer in the Union and argued in vain to prevent Texas from seceding.

What Democratic representative from Pennsylvania proposed in 1846 that slavery should be prohibited in the land acquired as a result of the Mexican War?

David Wilmot. His proposal was adopted in the House but defeated in the Senate.

Debate over the Compromise of 1850 was so heated that one Democrat pointed a pistol at another Democrat on the Senate floor. Who were these senators?

Senator Henry S. Foote of Mississippi drew his pistol, cocked it, and aimed at his longtime rival, Senator Thomas Hart Benton of Missouri, when Benton angrily approached him during the debate. Benton ripped his shirt open and shouted, "Let the assassin fire! He knows that I am not armed." Other senators seized the two men, and no shots were fired.

What cause that Benton vigorously championed finally came to fruition after his death?

He strongly supported the rapid development of the West and laws designed to help poor people obtain Western lands easily. His goal was realized, after his death, in the passage of the Homestead Acts.

Who was the only person to represent three different states in the Senate?

Democrat James Shields, who served in the Senate from Illinois for six years, from Minnesota for one year, and from Missouri for 39 days, between 1849 and 1879.

The archetype of corrupt, big-city political bosses served one term in the House. Who was he?

William M. "Boss" Tweed of Tammany Hall in New York City. During Tweed's short congressional career from 1853 to 1855, he was able to get Congress to pass a bill purchasing chairs from one of his relatives.

The most severe assault in the history of Congress was committed by what Southern congressman against what Northern senator?

In 1856 South Carolina Representative Preston Brooks was so angered by an antislavery speech by Senator Charles Sumner of Massachusetts that he entered the Senate chamber and beat Sumner in the head with a heavy cane until it broke. (Sumner was so badly injured that he could not return to the Senate for more than three years.) Brooks survived expulsion charges from the House through failure to muster the necessary two-thirds vote, but he resigned from office—only to be triumphantly reelected.

In 1858 Stephen Douglas and Abraham Lincoln engaged in a memorable series of debates. What office were they both running for?

A Senate seat from Illinois. Douglas won reelection to the Senate, but Lincoln's eloquence brought him national attention for the first time.

Who was the first Jewish senator?

David L. Julee of Florida, who joined other Southern senators in walking out when their states seceded in 1861.

What post-Civil War senator from Mississippi took courageous stands that most of his constituents opposed?

Lucius Quintus Cincinnatus Lamar. The Mississippi senator eulogized abolitionist Charles Sumner on the Senate floor when Sumner died. Later, even though the Mississippi legislature ordered all of its congressional delegation to vote in favor of the unlimited coinage of free silver, Lamar refused to do so.

Only once from 1859 to the end of the nineteenth century did Democrats control the presidency and both houses of Congress. At that time were many major laws enacted?

No. Grover Cleveland, who opposed free silver, and the Democratic Congress of 1893-94 quarreled so adamantly over this issue that party loyalty was lost. The President even accused Democratic congressmen of "party perfidy and party dishonor" when they failed to write strong tariff reforms.

In 1910 the Speaker of the House's enormous power finally was broken by rule changes that were supported by Democrats and

insurgent Republicans. What Democratic representative helped lead this fight?

James B. "Champ" Clark of Missouri, who became the next House Speaker in 1911.

What Democratic senators from Montana led the investigations of scandals in the Harding administration?

Thomas J. Walsh conducted the lengthy Senate investigation that laid bare the Teapot Dome and Elk Hills oil scandals. Burton K. Wheeler chaired the Senate committee that exposed the corruption and favoritism in the Justice Department headed by Attorney General Harry Daugherty, Harding's former campaign manager.

Who was the first Democratic congresswoman?

Mary T. Norton of New Jersey, who served from 1925 to 1951 and chaired three House committees.

Who was the first woman elected to the Senate?

Democrat Hattie W. Caraway of Arkansas. In 1931 she was appointed to fill a vacancy in the Senate caused by the death of her husband, and in the following year Mrs. Caraway was elected to a full six-year term. She stayed in the Senate until 1945.

Were any of William Jennings Bryan's descendants elected to Congress?

Yes. His daughter, Ruth Bryan Owen, served two terms as a congresswoman from Florida from 1929 to 1933.

More important laws were enacted in the "first hundred days" of Franklin D. Roosevelt's administration than in any other comparable period in Congress's history. Who were the leaders that pushed the New Deal legislation through Congress?

The Senate majority leader was Joseph T. Robinson of Arkansas, who persuaded Senate Democrats to bind themselves to vote with the party caucus's majority will. Speaker Henry T. Rainey of Illinois and Majority Leader Joseph W. Byrns of Tennessee controlled the House Democratic Caucus, the Rules Committee, and the Ways and Means Committee. They were able to push New Deal bills through the House under rules that severely limited debate and amendments.

What Southern senator broke with the New Deal because he felt that it was too conservative and that Franklin D. Roosevelt was an instrument of the plutocratic ruling class?

Huey Long of Louisiana, who proposed a radical "Share Our Wealth" program in which large fortunes would be confiscated and every family given enough money to have a house, a car, and a radio. Long, who entered the Senate in 1932, threatened to run against FDR in the 1936 presidential election, but he was assassinated in 1935.

The most important labor law passed during the New Deal period was the National Labor Relations Act, which required companies to allow workers to vote on union membership. What senator sponsored this legislation?

Robert Wagner of New York, who served in the Senate from 1927 to 1949.

One of the last major New Deal measures, the Fair Labor Standards Bill, which established national maximum hours and minimum wages, became law in 1938. What Democratic congresswoman defied a powerful committee to get the bill before the House for a vote?

Mary T. Norton of New Jersey, who outmaneuvered the Southern-dominated Rules Committee with a discharge petition signed by 218 representatives.

What Democratic representative kept probing the mysteriously padded wartime defense budget until finally the Secretary of War took him to Oak Ridge, Tennessee, and told him about the secret atomic bomb?

Clarence Cannon of Missouri, chairman of the House Appropriations Committee. Cannon and four of his committee members were taken to Oak Ridge; later the leaders of both parties in Congress were also told about the atom bomb. All of them kept it secret until the bombing of Hiroshima in 1945.

Who headed the special Senate committee that investigated the efficiency and fairness of World War II defense contracts?

Harry Truman, who served in the Senate from 1935 to 1945. Truman was not widely known before his appointment to this committee, but he gained a national reputation for successfully uncovering waste and inefficiency in the national defense program.

What Democrat was Speaker of the House longer than anyone else in our history?

Sam Rayburn of Texas, who was House Speaker for 17 years (1940-47, 1949-53, 1955-61). Rayburn started his long career as a congressman in 1913, the same year that Woodrow Wilson entered the White House. He did not leave his Capitol desk until shortly before his death in 1961, when John F. Kennedy was President.

Who sponsored the 1943 resolutions in the Senate and House that signaled bipartisan support for a world peacekeeping organization following World War II?

The Senate resolution by Foreign Relations Committee Chairman Tom Connally of Texas and the House resolution by freshman Representative J. William Fulbright of Arkansas put both houses squarely behind full participation by the United States in a postwar United Nations organization. Congressmen from both parties attended the 50-nation meeting at San Francisco where the United Nations Charter was signed in 1945.

Of which Georgia senator was it often said that he would have been elected President if he were not a Southerner?

Richard B. Russell, who served in the Senate from 1933 to 1971. As dean of the Southern senators Russell often led their opposition to civil rights bills, and this diminished his popularity with voters in other sections of the country. His colleague in the Senate, Lyndon B. Johnson, once said that Russell would have easily won a secret vote among senators on the man best qualified to be President. Ironically, when Russell was offered the post of Senate majority leader in 1953, he turned it down and suggested Lyndon B. Johnson for the job—thus putting a fellow Southerner on the road to the presidency.

Why was Lyndon B. Johnson such a strong Senate majority leader?

He was exceptionally adept at persuading wavering senators to vote the way he wanted. Also, he earned the respect and confidence of President Eisenhower and many Republicans in Congress. As majority leader he presided over the Democratic Policy Committee, which dictated the order and priority of legislation, and the Steering Committee, which made committee assignments. Johnson could make decisions that could mean life or death for legislation and success or failure for senators' careers.

Who was the oldest senator?

Theodore F. Green of Rhode Island. He was elected to the Senate in 1936 when he was 69. He served four terms and then retired at 93.

What congresswoman, the daughter of teachers and for 14 years a teacher herself, became the House's leader on education issues?

Edith Green of Oregon, who chaired the House Subcommittee on Education and played an important role in promoting every major education bill passed by Congress during her 20 years in the House.

What senator sponsored the bill that established the Peace Corps and was a leader in the civil rights movement for three decades?

Hubert Humphrey of Minnesota.

Did Hubert Humphrey return to the Senate after he had been Vice-President and had lost the presidential election in 1968?

Yes. Humphrey, who had served in the Senate from 1949 until he became Vice-President in 1965, was elected again to the Senate in 1970 and reelected by a three-to-one margin in 1976.

What senator, dying of a brain tumor and unable to speak, was wheeled into the chamber to record his crucial vote in favor of cloture during the floor fight over the 1964 Civil Rights Bill?

Democrat Clair Engle of California. He pointed at his eyes to indicate his "aye" vote.

Why was the first session of the 89th Congress, from January 4 to October 23, 1965, regarded as one of the most productive in American history?

This one session of Congress, during Lyndon B. Johnson's administration, passed 89 major bills. These included legislation for Medicare, aid to elementary, secondary, and college education, voting rights for minorities, antipoverty programs, housing and low-income rent supplements, a new Housing and Urban Development Cabinet department, water quality and air pollution controls, mass transit, an omnibus farm bill, public works, drug control, and a new National Foundation for the Arts and Humanities.

Who represented Arizona in Congress from the day it became a state in 1912 until 1969?

Carl Hayden. He served in the House until 1927 and then in the Senate, where, from 1957 on, he stood third in line to the presidency as president *pro tempore* of the Senate. The Senate traditionally gives this office to the majority party senator of longest seniority. Hayden retired at 91 and lived for another four years.

What father and son, both prominent Maryland senators, lost their Senate seats at the height of their careers?

Millard and Joseph Tydings. The elder Millard Tydings was chairman of the Armed Services Committee until he was targeted for defeat in 1952 by the rabid followers of Wisconsin Senator Joseph McCarthy. One unsavory campaign tactic used by the McCarthyites was to print a phony picture of Tydings allegedly conversing with the head of the American Communist Party.

His son, Joseph Tydings, was a friend of the Kennedy family and considered a rising star in the Senate. But Tydings was opposed by the powerful gun lobby and lost the 1968 election after a single Senate term.

What former Rhodes Scholar sponsored in the Senate the 1946 law which set up an international educational exchange program for graduate students?

J. William Fulbright of Arkansas, who was first elected to the Senate in 1944 and served five terms before being defeated in the 1974 Democratic primary by Governor Dale Bumpers.

Although he voted for the 1965 Tonkin Gulf Resolution that gave President Lyndon B. Johnson almost blanket authority to escalate the Vietnam War, Fulbright soon became one of the leading critics of American involvement in Southeast Asia.

What two Democratic senators were the only members of Congress who voted against the crucial Tonkin Gulf Resolution?

Ernest Gruening of Alaska and Wayne Morse of Oregon. They incurred the wrath of President Johnson, who described the issue as "supporting our boys overseas." The House voted 414-0 for the resolution.

Who said, "I need my conscience more than the President needs my vote," when he cast one of only three votes in the Senate against increased funding for the war in Vietnam in 1966?

Senator Gaylord Nelson of Wisconsin, who joined Morse and Gruening in this vote.

What other senators became outspoken critics of the Vietnam War?

In 1968 Senator Eugene McCarthy of Minnesota and Robert Kennedy ran in Democratic presidential primary elections as "peace candidates." By 1971 Democratic Senators Mike Mansfield of Montana, Frank Church of Idaho, and George McGovern of South Dakota and Republican Senators Mark Hatfield of Oregon, John Sherman Cooper of Kentucky, and Edward Brooke of Massachusetts had all sponsored antiwar resolutions.

In 1973, over President Richard Nixon's veto, Congress passed the War Powers Act, which prohibited presidential commitment of American military forces in other countries for more than 60 days without congressional authorization.

What Missouri congresswoman paid special attention to consumer protection and was the House sponsor of the Truth-in-Lending Act and the Food Stamp Program?

Leonor Sullivan of St. Louis, who served in the House from 1953 to 1977 and struggled unsuccessfully to have Congress enact an omnibus consumer protection law to unify what she considered scattergun federal regulations concerning food, drugs, cosmetics, banking, and credit.

What father, mother, and son successively held the same seat in Congress from 1933 to 1973?

John, Elizabeth, and James Kee of West Virginia.

Who was elected to the House of Representatives in 1946 and served as Speaker from 1971 to 1977?

Carl Albert of Oklahoma.

At no time in recent years has Congress been so dramatically on view to the public as in the televised Senate Watergate hearings which led to the resignation of President Nixon. Who were the senators that conducted this investigation?

The chairman was Democrat Sam J. Ervin of North Carolina,

and the vice-chairman was Republican Howard Baker of Tennessee. Other Democratic members of the committee were Daniel Inouye of Hawaii, Joseph Montoya of New Mexico, and Herman Talmadge of Georgia. Other Republican members were Edward Gurney of Florida and Lowell Weicker of Connecticut.

Who led the Watergate hearings in the House?

Chairman Peter Rodino of New Jersey led the Permanent Committee on the Judiciary, which voted for three articles of impeachment of President Nixon at the climax of its televised hearings in summer 1974.

What former Texas congresswoman impressed a national television audience with her eloquence at the House Watergate hearings?

Barbara C. Jordan, who left the House in 1979 to teach courses, including political values and ethics, at the University of Texas's Lyndon B. Johnson School of Public Affairs.

What Missouri representative battled the insider "establishment" throughout his 34 years in the House and capped his career by becoming Rules Committee chairman for four years?

Richard Bolling of Kansas City, who was a congressman from 1949 to 1983. Author of two widely admired books, *House Out of Order* (1965) and *Power in the House* (1968), Bolling led the fight for reforms in House procedures, including the election of committee chairmen and a new budget procedure.

The newest congressional building in Washington, D.C., is the Hart Senate Office Building. After whom is it named?

Philip Hart of Michigan, who served in the Senate from 1959 until 1976. Often called "the conscience of the Senate," Hart ranked near the top of colleague and press polls to select the most admired senator. Hart was Senate floor leader for the Civil Rights Act of 1968 that pertained to open housing. After 31 consecutive days of debate on this single bill, Hart finally succeeded in pushing it through the Senate.

What Connecticut woman was elected to Congress and then to her state's governorship by campaigning against the "cancer of depression" in Northeastern industrial cities?

Ella Grasso. Tragically, after four years in Congress and six years as governor, she lost her own fight against cancer and died in 1981.

The Equal Rights Amendment for women had been submitted to Congress without success each year since 1943. What Michigan congresswoman led the fight for the ERA in 1972 when it finally was passed by both houses of Congress?

Martha Griffiths, who served in the House from 1955 to 1975. House Minority Leader Gerald Ford called the ERA "a monument to Martha."

What black congressman from Illinois was elected by huge margins to 14 successive terms in the House?

William Dawson, whose tenure in the House began in 1943 and ended in 1971.

Who was the first black woman elected to Congress?

Shirley Chisholm, who was first elected to the House from Brooklyn, New York, in 1968. She left Congress in 1981 and became a professor at Mount Holyoke College.

What feminist leader who usually wore a hat served three terms in the House?

Bella Abzug, who represented a New York district in the House from 1971 to 1977. She gave up her House seat to run unsuccessfully for the Senate in 1976.

What son of a Democratic presidential nominee served from 1970 to 1981 as an Illinois senator?

Adlai E. Stevenson III.

Who served 16 years as Senate majority leader, retired from Congress in 1977, and then became United States ambassador to Japan?

Mike Mansfield of Montana.

What senator was called by President Carter "the most beloved of all Americans" at his 1977 funeral?

Hubert Humphrey of Minnesota.

RECENT LEADERS
IN CONGRESS

The same congressional district in what state has been represented successively by a President and a Speaker of the House of Representatives?

The Eighth District of Massachusetts was represented from 1947 to 1953 by John F. Kennedy and since 1953 by Thomas P. "Tip" O'Neill, Jr. O'Neill began his tenure as Speaker of the House in 1977.

Who is the House majority leader?

Representative Jim Wright of Texas, who has been in the House since 1955 and has been majority leader since 1977.

Who is the Senate minority leader?

Robert C. Byrd of West Virginia, who has held this position since the Republicans gained control of the Senate following the 1980 elections. Byrd was Senate majority leader during the four years of the Carter administration.

Is Robert Byrd a member of the famous family that dominated Virginia politics for many years?

No. He was born in poverty and raised after his mother's death as a foster child in a poor West Virginia mining town.

What Democrat was first elected to the Senate in 1972 when he was only 29 years old?

Joseph Biden, Jr., of Delaware. He became 30, which is the minimum age for senators, before his term began.

What Illinois congressman is chairman of the powerful House Ways and Means Committee?

Dan Rostenkowski, who has been in the House since 1959.

What Democratic senator issues "Golden Fleece" awards to persons and organizations that he feels are wasting federal money?

William Proxmire of Wisconsin. Three times in the 1950s Proxmire ran for governor of Wisconsin, and each time he lost; six times (beginning in 1957) he ran for a Senate seat, and each time he won.

What Illinois congressman retired from the House after he was elected mayor of one of the nation's largest cities in 1983?

Harold Washington, who became mayor of Chicago.

What Georgia Democrat is probably the single most influential senator on military affairs?

Sam Nunn, who was first elected to the Senate in 1972.

The city of Baltimore, Maryland, is represented in the House by what Polish-American woman?

Barbara A. Mikulski, who won her first election to Congress in 1976.

The city with the largest percentage of Mexican-Americans in the United States is represented by what congressman?

San Antonio, Texas, is represented by Henry B. Gonzalez, who has served in the House since 1963.

What Rhode Island senator sponsored legislation to provide federal grants to help students pay for their college education?

Claiborne Pell, who has served in the Senate since 1961. The former "Basic Educational Opportunity Grant" is now called a "Pell Grant" in his honor.

What liberal senator is a Rhodes Scholar of Greek descent?

Paul Sarbanes of Maryland, who was elected to the Senate in 1976 and reelected in 1982.

California's 23rd Congressional District—one of the most affluent in the nation—was once represented by liberal Helen Gahagan Douglas, whom Richard Nixon smeared as the "pink lady" when they ran for the Senate in 1950. Is this wealthy district now represented by a Democrat?

Yes. Since 1977 this heavily Jewish section of greater Los Angeles has been represented by Harvard-educated Anthony C. Beilenson, whom many regard as one of the most intelligent and hardworking members of the House.

In 1970 Vice-President George Bush ran for the Senate and lost. The Democrat who defeated him was reelected to his third Senate term in 1982. Who is he?

Lloyd Bentsen of Texas.

What senator was both a Rhodes Scholar and a pro basketball player with the New York Knicks?

Bill Bradley of New Jersey.

What Oklahoma congressman is chairman of the House Budget Committee?

James R. Jones, who was first elected to the House in 1972.

What longtime Southern senator is the son of a powerful populist politician whose nickname was "Kingfish"?

Russell Long, the son of Huey Long, who ruled as the virtual king of Louisiana from 1929 until he was assassinated in 1935. Russell Long was first elected to the Senate in 1948, the same year that Harry Truman won his upset victory over Thomas E. Dewey.

Both Democratic senators from what Southwestern state previously had been governors of that state?

Dale Bumpers was governor of Arkansas from 1970 to 1974 before being elected to the Senate in 1974. David Pryor was

governor of Arkansas from 1975 to 1978 before being elected
to the Senate in 1978.

**What California congressman of Spanish descent has served in
the House for more than 20 years?**
Edward R. Roybal, who was first elected to the House in 1962.

**What Japanese-American senator, who lost an arm in World
War II, has been in Congress ever since Hawaii became a state?**
Daniel K. Inouye, who served in the House from 1959 to
1963 and in the Senate since 1963.

Is Hawaii's other senator also a Japanese-American Democrat?
Yes. He is Spark M. Matsunaga, who first won his Senate seat
in 1976 when Chinese-American Hiram L. Fong, a Republican
senator, did not run for another term.

**What congresswoman from Louisiana was elected to the House
after her husband was killed in an airplane crash?**
Corinne "Lindy" Boggs was first elected in a 1973 special
election to the House seat that had been held by Majority Leader
Hale Boggs until his death in October 1972. Representative
Boggs served as permanent chairperson of the 1976 Democratic
convention.

**Another woman was elected to the House after her husband had
won the Democratic congressional nomination and then was
killed in a plane crash. Who is she?**
Marilyn Lloyd of Tennessee, who was first elected to the
House in 1974.

**What Democratic senator had been a domestic adviser to President Nixon and United States ambassador to the United Nations
in President Ford's administration?**
Daniel Patrick Moynihan of New York.

**What swing voter provided the crucial vote that guaranteed
Senate ratification of the Panama Canal Treaties in Carter's
administration?**
Democratic Senator Dennis DeConcini of Arizona.

What Rocky Mountain state gave 53 percent of its vote to Gerald Ford in 1976 and 57 percent to Ronald Reagan in 1980 but had two Democratic senators in 1984?

Montana, whose Democratic senators are John Melcher and Max Baucus.

The son of what former senator from a New England state is now a senator from that same state?

Christopher Dodd, the son of Thomas Dodd, is a senator from Connecticut. The elder Dodd lost his race for reelection in 1970, and exactly one decade later Christopher Dodd was elected to the Senate.

What Democrat unseated an incumbent senator, who then became national chairman of the Republican Party?

James Sasser of Tennessee defeated Senator Bill Brock in 1976 and was reelected in 1982.

What former Rhodes Scholar was governor of Oklahoma before he was elected to the Senate?

David L. Boren.

Who became the dean of the Congressional Black Caucus because his tenure in the House dated back to 1963?

Augustus Hawkins of Los Angeles, California. During Carter's administration he was the House sponsor of the Humphrey-Hawkins Bill to provide more jobs for the unemployed.

Why did John Glenn have to drop out of his first Senate race in 1964?

The first American astronaut to orbit the earth slipped in a bathroom and was stricken with severe vertigo. He was elected to the Senate from Ohio in 1974 and reelected in 1980 by more than a three-to-one margin at the same time that Ronald Reagan was carrying Ohio comfortably.

Did Howard Metzenbaum, Ohio's other Democratic senator, ever run in a primary race against John Glenn?

Yes, twice. In 1970 he defeated Glenn for the Democratic Senate nomination, but Metzenbaum lost the general election to Robert Taft, Jr. In 1974 Metzenbaum was appointed to fill a Senate vacancy. Later that year he was defeated by Glenn in the Democratic primary election for a full six-year term. But Metzenbaum persisted, and finally in 1976 he was elected to the Senate and then reelected in 1982.

The minority whip in the Senate is a fast runner. When he was in his sixties he set the 100-yard dash record for his age group. Who is he?

Alan Cranston of California.

When presidential nominee George McGovern dropped Senator Thomas Eagleton as his running mate in 1972, did this foreshadow the end of Eagleton's political career?

No. The people of Missouri returned Eagleton to the Senate in 1974 with 60 percent of the vote, and they elected him to a third term in 1980, even though Ronald Reagan carried the state in the presidential race.

For the first time in its history Nebraska has two Democratic senators. Who are they?

Edward Zorinsky and J. James Exon. Nebraska is a predominantly Republican state, and both its senators (especially Zorinsky) are more conservative than most of their Midwestern colleagues.

Following the 1980 elections the Republicans gained control of the Senate for the first time in 26 years. How many additional Senate seats did the GOP pick up in 1980?

Twelve.

Did the Republicans also regain control of the House of Representatives after the 1980 elections?

No. The Republicans gained 33 seats in the House, but the Democrats still maintained control, 243 to 192.

What four-term senator from Idaho, who headed the powerful Senate Foreign Relations Committee, fell victim in 1980 to the Republican blitz?

Frank Church, who was ousted from office by Congressman Steven Symms.

In 1980, what former Democratic presidential nominee lost his race for a fourth term in the Senate?

George McGovern of South Dakota, who was defeated by Congressman James Abdnor.

What liberal Indiana senator, who had sponsored bills to reform the method of electing the President, was another loser in 1980?

Birch Bayh. When he first ran for the Senate in 1962 against three-term incumbent Homer Capehart, Bayh admonished voters that "18 years in Washington is enough for one man." This advice came back to haunt Bayh in 1980 when he was seeking a fourth term, and he lost his Senate seat to Congressman Dan Quayle.

What Democratic senator from Colorado barely survived the 1980 Republican avalanche?

Gary Hart, who was reelected to the Senate by about 19,000 votes out of more than 1,160,000 votes that were cast.

What New Jersey senator resigned in 1982 after being convicted of accepting bribes as part of the Abscam scandal?

Harrison Williams. (Abscam was the FBI agents' nickname for their undercover operation in which an agent posed as an Arab sheik and offered bribes in front of hidden TV cameras to some members of Congress.)

In the 1982 elections, when the presidency was not at stake, did the Democrats' lead in the House shrink or expand?

The Democrats picked up 26 additional seats in 1982 to expand their lead in the House to 269 to 166.

In which state did the Democrats make their largest net gain in the 1982 House elections?

In California, where the Democrats had a net gain of six more seats. The nation's largest state then had a House delegation of 28 Democrats and 17 Republicans.

Did the Democrats also pick up additional Senate seats in the 1982 election?

No. After the 1982 elections there were 54 Republicans and still only 46 Democrats in the Senate. (The Republicans increased their number of senators to 55 in September 1983, when Democratic Senator Henry Jackson of Washington died and the vacancy was filled by Republican Daniel Evans.)

Did any Democratic candidate defeat an incumbent Republican senator in 1982?

Yes. New Mexico Attorney General Jeff Bingaman unseated Republican Senator Harrison Schmitt.

In the 1982 elections were a large number of incumbents in Congress defeated in their bids for reelection?

No. Of the 382 Democrats and Republicans running for reelection, only 29 (26 Republicans and 3 Democrats) were defeated.

What North Dakota Democrat at the age of 74 was elected in 1982 to another term in the Senate?

Quentin Burdick.

Due to redistricting in Massachusetts two incumbents ran for one house seat in 1982. Who won?

Freshman Democrat Barney Frank defeated eight-term Republican Margaret Heckler.

The most surprising Senate race in 1982 occurred in New Jersey. What happened there?

Democrat Frank Lautenberg defeated popular Congresswoman Millicent Fenwick, who was the inspiration for Lacey Davenport in the comic strip "Doonesbury." Lautenberg, who helped build a five-man business-machine firm into a company with 16,000 employees that grossed $669 million in 1981, had never run for public office before.

When Edmund S. Muskie resigned from the Senate in May 1980 to become Jimmy Carter's Secretary of State, his vacancy was filled by Democrat George R. Mitchell. Was Mitchell elected in 1982 to a six-year Senate term?

Yes.

Democratic Congressman Lawrence McDonald of Georgia, who was chairman of the John Birch Society, was killed when the

Soviets shot down a Korean airliner on September 1, 1983. His wife Kathy ran in a special election to complete her conservative husband's term. Was she elected?

No. Moderate Democrat George "Buddy" Darden was elected to this House seat.

In 1984, who had the longest tenure of any Democratic woman in Congress?

Patricia Schroeder of Colorado, who was first elected to the House in 1972.

What senator holds the all-time record for consecutive roll-call votes?

William Proxmire of Wisconsin, who by 1979 had surpassed Margaret Chase Smith's prior record of 2,941 consecutive roll-calls.

Who was the oldest member of Congress in 1984?

Representative Claude Pepper of Florida, who was born September 8, 1900. Pepper served in the Senate from 1937 to 1951 and has been a member of the House since 1963. A leading spokesman for the interests of senior citizens, Pepper succeeded in having Congress enact a law to change the mandatory retirement age from 65 to 70 for most jobs.

In 1984 the Republicans had to win back the 26 House seats they lost in 1982 to give them the conservative majority needed to pass bills favored by President Reagan. Did they achieve this goal in the 1984 House elections?

No. The GOP gained only 14 seats, which meant that the House would still be dominated by liberals and moderates.

The Democrats needed six additional seats to regain control of the Senate. Did they win these six seats in 1984?

No. Their net gain was only two seats, which gave the Democrats 47 senators to the Republicans' 53.

In 1984 Democrats defeated which two Republican senators in their bids for reelection?

In Illinois Representative Paul Simon unseated Charles Percy, an 18-year Senate veteran, and in Iowa Congressman Thomas Harkin defeated Senator Roger Jepsen.

What Democratic son-in-law of a defeated GOP senator won the Senate seat vacated in 1984 by Jennings Randolph?

John D. "Jay" Rockefeller IV of West Virginia, whose father-in-law is Charles Percy.

What two other seats vacated by retiring senators were won by Democrats?

Lieutenant Governor John Kerry of Massachusetts was elected to replace retiring Senator Paul Tsongas, and in Tennessee Howard Baker's seat went to Congressman Albert Gore, Jr., whose father had been a popular Tennessee senator from 1953 to 1971.

Who was the only Democratic senator defeated in 1984?

Walter "Dee" Huddleston of Kentucky was ousted by Judge Mitch McConnell, whose winning margin was about 4,000 votes out of nearly 1.3 million cast.

What ultraconservative GOP senator was reelected in the most expensive Senate race in history?

Jesse Helms of North Carolina, the dean of the New Right in the Senate, who defeated Governor James Hunt in a hard-fought election that cost about $23 million.

What Democratic incumbent senators were reelected in 1984?

Howell Heflin of Alabama, David Pryor of Arkansas, Joseph Biden, Jr., of Delaware, Sam Nunn of Georgia, J. Bennett Johnston, Jr., of Louisiana, Carl Levin of Michigan, Max Baucus of Montana, J. James Exon of Nebraska, Bill Bradley of New Jersey, David Boren of Oklahoma, and Claiborne Pell of Rhode Island.

SLOGANS

With what early President do we associate the slogan "To the Victor Belong the Spoils"?

Andrew Jackson, who was charged with removing many federal employees from office. As President he replaced 252 out of a total 612 officers (not counting postmasters). However, Abraham Lincoln used the spoils system more than Jackson did. Lincoln replaced 1,457 federal workers, leaving less than 200 from previous administrations.

"Fifty-four Forty or Fight!" was a popular slogan during James K. Polk's administration. To what did it refer?

It referred to the struggle with Great Britain over the boundary of the Oregon Country. American expansionists wanted the border to extend northward to 54°40' on the map, which was the southern boundary of Alaska. But our government and the British finally compromised in 1846 and set the border along the 49th parallel.

What pun was popular with the Democrats in the 1852 presidential campaign?

"We Polked 'em in '44; we'll Pierce 'em in '52."

"Buck and Breck" was a favorite slogan in the election of 1856. To what two Democrats did it refer?

Presidential candidate James Buchanan and vice-presidential candidate John C. Breckinridge.

What were some of the Democratic slogans in 1864, when General George McClellan tried to unseat President Abraham Lincoln during the Civil War?

"Mac Will Win the Union Back," "Abolish Old Abe and Restore the Union," "Abe Lincoln, First in War and First in the Pockets of His Countrymen," and "Lincoln Demands Blood, the People Demand Peace."

What slogans following the disputed election of 1876 indicated that some Democrats would rather fight than accept the decision that Samuel J. Tilden would not be President?

"Tilden or Fight," "Tilden or Blood," and "On to Washington." For many years afterward Democrats referred to the election as the "Great Fraud" and the "Crime of '76."

What was the meaning of the Democrats' 1896 campaign slogan, "Sixteen to One"?

It reflected William Jennings Bryan's belief that the government should permit the free and unlimited coinage of silver at the rate of 16 ounces of silver to 1 ounce of gold.

"A Republic Can Have No Colonies" and "The Flag of a Republic Forever, of an Empire Never" were Democratic slogans in what presidential campaign?

These were slogans in 1900 when William Jennings Bryan opposed the United States keeping the Philippine Islands, which had been taken from Spain as a result of the Spanish-American War.

Who created the famous slogan "What This Country Needs Is a Good Five-cent Cigar"?

Thomas R. Marshall, who was Vice-President in Woodrow Wilson's administration.

"He Kept Us Out of War" was the Democrats' chief slogan when Wilson was running for reelection in November 1916.

What was ironic about this slogan?

Five months later, in April 1917, the United States entered World War I.

"Happy Days Are Here Again" has virtually become the anthem of the Democratic Party. It was first played and sung in what election campaign?

In the 1932 campaign, when Franklin D. Roosevelt was seeking his first term in the White House. (It had been introduced two years earlier in the movie musical *Chasing Rainbows*.) The Democrats had some clever slogans in 1932, such as "In Hoover We Trusted, Now We Are Busted" and "Roosevelt or Ruin."

In what election campaign did the Democrats revive a slogan that the Republicans had used when Lincoln was running for reelection during the Civil War?

In 1940, when Roosevelt was seeking a third term and war clouds were threatening the country, Democrats cried out, "Don't Swap Horses in Midstream."

How did the slogan "Give 'em Hell, Harry" originate?

Harry Truman delivered hundreds of brief rear-platform speeches in his 1948 "whistle-stop" campaign that took him by train to many parts of the country. In Seattle a man in the crowd shouted, "Give 'em hell, Harry." Truman shot back, "I have never deliberately given anybody hell. I just tell the truth on the opposition—and they think it's hell."

What were some of the popular slogans that rhymed with Adlai Stevenson's first name?

"We're Madly for Adlai," "We Need Adlai Badly," and "Vote Gladly for Adlai."

What was the best-known slogan when Lyndon B. Johnson ran against Barry Goldwater in 1964?

"All the Way with LBJ." Perhaps the Democrats' most humorous slogan in that campaign was a parody on the Republicans' rather sanctimonious statement about Goldwater—"In Your Heart You Know He's Right." To this the Democrats answered, "In Your Guts You Know He's Nuts."

In 1972 George McGovern used an expression in his speech accepting the Democratic presidential nomination that became a campaign slogan. What was it?

"Come Home, America."

The title of what book was used as a slogan when Jimmy Carter campaigned for the presidency?

Why Not the Best?, which was written by Carter himself.

When Walter Mondale and Gary Hart were competing for the 1984 presidential nomination, Mondale countered Hart's attack with what humorous slogan?

"Where's the Beef?" This slogan was copied from a popular TV commercial that advertised a chain of fast-food restaurants.

NICKNAMES

Who were the three Democratic Presidents whose best-known nicknames were their initials?

Franklin Delano Roosevelt "FDR," John Fitzgerald Kennedy "JFK," and Lyndon Baines Johnson "LBJ."

How did Thomas Jefferson get the nicknames of "Long Tom" and "Red Fox"?

He was 6 feet 2½ inches tall, and his hair was reddish.

What President richly deserved the nickname "Father of the Constitution"?

James Madison.

What President was called the "Last of the Cocked Hats"?

James Monroe.

What President acquired his most popular nickname after he left the White House?

John Quincy Adams, who was called "Old Man Eloquent" because of the impassioned speeches he delivered as a congressman following his presidency.

His friends called Andrew Jackson the "People's President," and his enemies called him "King Andrew the First," but what was his best-known nickname?

"Old Hickory."

What President was known by a host of nicknames, including the "Little Magician," "Flying Dutchman," "American Talleyrand," "Wizard of Kinderhook" (his New York home), and "Mistletoe Politician"?

Martin Van Buren.

Who was called "Young Hickory" and "Napoleon of the Stump"?

James K. Polk.

Another President was called "Young Hickory of the Granite Hills" and "Handsome Frank." Who was he?

Franklin Pierce of New Hampshire.

Who was the "Little Giant"?

Senator Stephen A. Douglas of Illinois, who was about 5 feet 1 inch tall.

The most reluctant presidential candidate in history was Horatio Seymour. What was his famous nickname?

"The Great Decliner."

Why was Horace Greeley called "Old White Coat and Hat"?

One of Greeley's eccentricities was his attire; he nearly always wore a shabby old white coat and a high white hat.

How did Grover Cleveland acquire the nickname "Veto President"?

In his first term in the White House, Cleveland vetoed 413 bills, which was more than twice the number of vetoes exercised by his 21 predecessors, from Washington to Arthur.

Who was the "Boy Orator of the Platte"?

William Jennings Bryan. Republicans responded to this nickname with the exaggeration that the Platte River in Nebraska was "six inches deep and a mile wide at the mouth."

What were Woodrow Wilson's chief nicknames?

"Schoolmaster President," "Scholar in Politics," and "Professor."

Who was the "Happy Warrior," and how did he get this nickname?

Alfred E. "Al" Smith, who was called the "Happy Warrior" by Franklin D. Roosevelt when he nominated Smith for the presidency at the Democratic convention in 1928.

How did his nicknames reveal that Franklin D. Roosevelt was a highly controversial President?

His friends called him "Champ," "Boss," the "Squire of Hyde Park," and the "Wizard in the White House." His enemies referred to FDR as "Dictator," "Socialist," and "That Man in the White House." Father Charles E. Coughlin, a demagogue who admired Hitler, called the New Deal President "Franklin Double-crossing Roosevelt."

Who was "Cactus Jack"?

Texas-born John Nance Garner, who served as Vice-President during Franklin D. Roosevelt's first two terms in the White House.

In what two ways was "Man of Independence" an appropriate nickname for Harry Truman?

Truman hailed from Independence, Missouri, and he was an outspoken President whom no one could intimidate.

Who was the "Veep"?

Alben W. Barkley, who was Vice-President from 1949 to 1953 in Truman's administration.

His family and friends called John F. Kennedy by what nickname?

"Jack."

Lyndon B. Johnson was given a sarcastic nickname after he won a close and controversial Senate primary race in 1948. Later this same nickname described the size of his victory over Barry Goldwater in the 1964 presidential election. What was it?

"Landslide Lyndon."

What Democrat who ran against Richard Nixon for the presidency was sometimes called the "Prairie Populist"?

George McGovern of South Dakota.

Who was called the "Man from Plains"?

Jimmy Carter, who came from the small town of Plains, Georgia and campaigned as a plain, down-to-earth man.

Do Walter Frederick Mondale's close friends and family call him Walt or Wally?

No. Mondale's nickname is "Fritz."

In 1984 there was a powerful new voting bloc called the "Yuppies." Who are they?

Young urban professionals.

WIT

One Southerner who felt only contempt for John Adams could scarcely believe that Adams had died on the same day that his hero, Thomas Jeffereson, had passed away. "It's a damned Yankee trick!" he sputtered.

* * * * *

When John Quincy Adams reached an old age, he described himself to a friend in this way: "I inhabit a weak, frail, decayed tenement, battered by the winds and broken in upon by the storms, and, from all I can learn, the landlord does not intend to repair."

* * * * *

Former President Andrew Jackson was angry when he learned that President James K. Polk had named James Buchanan as his Secretary of State. But Polk reminded Jackson, "You yourself appointed him minister to Russia in your first term."

"Yes, I did," replied Jackson. "It was as far as I could send him out of my sight and where he could do the least harm! I would have sent him to the North Pole if we had kept a minister there."

* * * * *

Martin Van Buren acquired a widespread reputation for straddling issues. Once a senator made a bet that he could force Van Buren to take a positive stand. "Mr. Van Buren," he said, "it's been rumored that the sun rises in the East. Do you believe it?"

"Well, Senator," answered Van Buren, "I understand that's the common acceptance, but as I never get up till after dawn, I can't really say."

* * * * *

Grover Cleveland had much better relations with the House of Representatives than with the Senate. One night he was awakened by his wife, who called out, "I think there are burglars in the house!"

"No, dear," grumbled Cleveland sleepily. "In the Senate maybe, but not in the House."

* * * * *

Once when William Jennings Bryan addressed a group of farmers, he had to climb on top of a manure spreader to be seen by the audience. "This is the first time," Bryan chuckled, "that I ever spoke from a Republican platform."

Another time Bryan told a rather hostile audience, "Tonight my beloved wife sleeps in a humble inn two miles from here, but come next March she will be sleeping in the White House."

Someone in the crowd snapped back, "Well, if she is, she'll be sleeping with McKinley because he's going to be the next man in the White House!"

* * * * *

Once when President Theodore Roosevelt was speaking before a crowd, an obstreperous individual kept shouting, "I am a Democrat! I am a Democrat!"

Finally Roosevelt replied, "If the gentleman is so eager to speak, why doesn't he tell us just why he is a Democrat?"

The man was glad to explain, "My granddaddy was a Democrat. My father was a Democrat. So I'm a Democrat!"

President Roosevelt beamed. "I have a question for you, sir. If your grandfather was a jackass and your father was a jackass, just what does that make you?"

The heckler was not to be outdone. "A Republican!" he roared.

* * * * *

When Woodrow Wilson was governor of New Jersey, he was informed that one of the state's senators had just died. A short time later Wilson received a call from an ambitious politician. "Governor," he said, "I would like to take the senator's place."

"Well," bristled the angry Wilson, "you may quote me as saying that's perfectly agreeable to me if it's agreeable to the undertaker."

* * * * *

One afternoon when Woodrow Wilson was playing golf, a boy at the edge of the course made repeated Indian calls. "That boy must be training to be a senator," Wilson snapped. "He is always making a noise with his mouth and not saying anything."

* * * * *

After Wilson suffered a stroke, Republican Senator Albert Fall of New Mexico paid a courtesy call on the partially paralyzed President. Wilson had little respect for Fall (who became Secretary of the Interior in Harding's administration and went to prison for his involvement in the Teapot Dome scandal). The Republican senator said to Wilson sanctimoniously, "We have all been praying for you, sir."

Wilson replied sarcastically, "Which way, Senator?"

* * * * *

Wilson's Vice-President, Thomas R. Marshall, didn't think much of his job. He wrote, "Once there were two brothers. One ran away to sea, the other was elected Vice-President, and nothing was ever heard of either of them again."

* * * * *

From the onset of the Great Depression until he left the White House, President Herbert Hoover was usually gloomy and forlorn. Gutzon Borglum, the sculptor, captured the essence of Hoover's dejection when he remarked, "If you put a rose in Hoover's hand it would wilt."

* * * * *

Franklin D. Roosevelt loved to tell this joke on himself. Every morning a Republican businessman who commuted to work by train bought a newspaper, glanced at the headlines, and then handed it back to the newsboy. One day the puzzled newsboy asked the businessman why he looked at only the first page. "I'm just interested in the obituary notices," he replied.

"But they're on page 24," said the newsboy, "and you never look at them."

"Boy," exclaimed the businessman, "the son-of-a-bitch I'm interested in will be on page one!"

* * * * *

When FDR appointed Frances Perkins as the first woman on a President's Cabinet, Mrs. Roosevelt sympathized with her husband for having to bicker with the labor leaders who wanted the position to go to a man. "Oh, that's all right," Roosevelt assured his wife, "I'd rather have trouble with them for an hour than trouble with you for the rest of my life!"

* * * * *

Roosevelt's cantankerous Secretary of the Interior Harold Ickes felt the President carried his devotion to the sea a bit too far when he called a Cabinet meeting aboard the *Indianapolis*. "I'm willing to die for the President," Ickes snarled, "but I won't get seasick for him."

* * * * *

For many years Maine held its elections before other states, which gave rise to the saying, "As Maine goes, so goes the nation." In the 1936 election Franklin D. Roosevelt carried every state except Maine and Vermont. This led to the quip: "As Maine goes, so goes Vermont."

* * * * *

Fontaine Maury Maverick, a Texas Democrat who served in Congress from 1935 to 1939, had been a World War I officer who was awarded the Silver Star and Purple Heart. But at a congressional hearing he was angered when a militaristic colleague kept badgering a woman witness who was a pacifist. "Who won the World War?" thundered the bellicose congressman.

At this point Maverick interrupted, "Who won the San Francisco earthquake?"

* * * * *

A friend once asked Harry Truman about the famous photograph showing him playing the piano with actress Lauren Bacall sitting on top of the piano. "What did Bess say when she saw the picture?" the friend inquired.

"Well," Truman replied, "she said maybe it was time for me to quit playing the piano."

* * * * *

Truman acquired a reputation for using earthy locker-room language that some critics claimed was too undignified for a President. A lady once told Bess Truman that she was horrified to hear the President refer to a politician's statement as "a bunch of horse manure."

Wearily Mrs. Truman replied, "You don't know how many years it took me to tone it down to that!"

* * * * *

While Truman was President a reporter asked Senator Margaret Chase Smith what she would do if she woke up one morning and found herself in the White House. "I'd go straight to Mrs. Truman and apologize," she replied. "Then I'd go home."

* * * * *

Adlai Stevenson was famous for his quips. In response to the charge that he was an intellectual egghead, he jovially replied, "Eggheads of the world, unite! You have nothing to lose but your yolks." Another time he declared, "If the Republicans stop telling lies about us, we will stop telling the truth about them." Although the presidency eluded him, Stevenson surmised, "In America any boy may become President, and I suppose that's just the risk he takes."

* * * * *

Once when Stevenson was making a speech at an outdoor rally, a page of his address was picked up by the wind and swept away. "Well," observed the presidential candidate as he looked at the audience, "that's one break for you."

* * * * *

Many stories were told about how millionaire Joseph P. Kennedy provided huge funds for son John's political campaigns. JFK joked about this with reporters, saying, "I have just received the following wire from my generous Daddy: 'Dear Jack, don't buy a single vote more than necessary. I'll be damned if I'm going to pay for a landslide.' "

* * * * *

Three of the Democrats who were potential presidential nominees in 1960 were Senators John F. Kennedy, Stuart Symington, and Lyndon B. Johnson. At a Gridiron Club dinner in 1958 Senator Kennedy told reporters this story: "I dreamed about 1960 myself the other night and I told Stuart Symington and Lyndon Johnson about it in the cloakroom yesterday. I told them how the Lord came into my bedroom, anointed my head, and said, 'John Kennedy, I hereby appoint you President of the United States.' Stuart Symington said, 'That's strange, Jack, because I too had a similar dream last night in which the Lord anointed me and declared me, Stuart Symington, President of the United States and Outer Space.' Lyndon Johnson said,

'That's very interesting, gentlemen, because I too had a similar dream last night and I don't remember anointing either of you.' "

* * * * *

Lyndon B. Johnson was setting an extremely hard pace for the legislature in 1959. One senator groaned, "Rome wasn't built in a day."

A fellow senator replied, "Yes, but Lyndon Johnson wasn't the architect on that job."

* * * * *

During the 1960 presidential campaign John F. Kennedy said, "Last Thursday night Mr. Nixon dismissed me as 'another Truman.' I regard that as a great compliment. I consider him another Dewey."

* * * * *

When Kennedy was confronted on the campaign trail about the question of his Catholicism, he sometimes told this anecdote: "I think it well that we recall what happened to a great governor when he became a presidential nominee. Despite his successful record, despite his plainspoken voice, the campaign was a debacle. His views were distorted. He carried fewer states than any candidate in his party's history. To top it off, he lost his own state that he had served so well." The audience expected Kennedy to name Al Smith as the subject of his story. Instead JFK continued, "You all know who he was, and I'm sure you remember his religion—Alfred M. Landon, Protestant."

* * * * *

Shortly after the election a woman in Kansas went to her local post office to get some stamps. When she asked for 50 cents' worth of stamps, the clerk inquired, "What denomination?"

"Well, I didn't know it had come to that," the woman said in amazement. "Baptist," she added.

* * * * *

When Governor Orville Freeman of Minnesota was asked why President Kennedy selected him as Secretary of Agriculture, Freeman replied, "I think it has something to do with the fact that Harvard doesn't have a school of agriculture."

* * * * *

While he was agonizing about the Cuban missile crisis of 1962, President Kennedy made a confession to Hubert Humphrey, who had dropped out of the race for the 1960 Democratic presidential nomination after JFK had beaten him in the West Virginia primary election. "If I'd known the job was this tough," Kennedy said, "I wouldn't have trounced you in West Virginia."

"If I hadn't known it was this tough, " Humphrey replied, "I never would have let you beat me."

* * * * *

Once after Vice-President Johnson described with awe the many brilliant persons President Kennedy had brought into the White House, Congressman Sam Rayburn remarked, "Well, Lyndon, they may be just as intelligent as you say. But I'd feel a helluva lot better if just one of them had ever run for sheriff."

* * * * *

Lyndon B. Johnson thrived on work, and he constantly prodded his staff to labor as hard as he did. "I don't have ulcers," he boasted. "I give 'em." Another time he said about his White House staff, "There are no favorites in my office. I treat them all with the same general inconsideration."

* * * * *

Hubert Humphrey once said the following about his political ambitions: "I'm like the girl next door—always available but you don't necessarily think about marriage."

* * * * *

During the 1964 campaign Humphrey told a group of students who were supporting Barry Goldwater, "I don't care if you study ancient history, but don't vote for it."

* * * * *

After Attorney General Robert Kennedy decided to run for the Senate from New York in 1964, some critics complained that he did so at the request of the state's "bosses." Crowds jammed the lobby of one New York hotel where Kennedy was staying. He smiled at the hundreds of people and quipped, "I am delighted to see so many bosses here to welcome me."

* * * * *

Once when President Lyndon B. Johnson was about to take a helicopter flight from a military airport, an army sergeant noticed that the President was heading for the wrong helicopter. He rushed up to LBJ and exclaimed, "Mr. President, *that* is your helicopter over there." Johnson put his arm on the soldier's shoulder and replied, "Son, they are *all* my helicopters."

* * * * *

Former Congressman Emanuel Celler of New York had just delivered a speech at a political rally. One woman in the audience gushed, "Oh, Mr. Celler, your speech was positively marvelous. I would so like to have a copy."

Celler explained that he was sorry but had not prepared a text. "Do you think your speech will ever be printed?" she asked.

"Posthumously, perhaps," he replied wryly.

"Oh, wonderful!" she beamed. "I do hope it will be soon."

* * * * *

Jimmy Carter's mother, whose fancies included baseball, TV soap operas, and a nightly swig of bourbon, said she had no regrets when her son was defeated by Ronald Reagan in 1980. "I never did like the White House," Miss Lillian asserted. "It was boring."

BIBLIOGRAPHY

Adler, Bill. *The Washington Wits.* New York: Macmillan, 1967.

Aikman, Lonnelle. *The Living White House.* Washington: White House Historical Association, 1982.

Alexander, Herbert E. *Financing Politics: Money, Elections and Political Reforms.* Washington: Congressional Quarterly Press, 1980.

Bailey, Thomas A. *Voices of America: The Nation's Story in Slogans, Sayings, and Songs.* New York: The Free Press, 1976.

Barber, James David. *The Pulse of Politics: Electing Presidents in the Media Age.* New York: Norton, 1980.

Barone, Michael, and Grant Ujifusa. *The Almanac of American Politics, 1984.* Washington: National Journal, 1983.

Bates, E.S. *The Story of Congress, 1789-1935.* New York: Harper, 1936.

Binkley, Wilfred E. *President and Congress,* 3rd ed. New York: Vintage Books, 1962.

Boller, Paul F., Jr. *Presidential Anecdotes.* New York: Oxford University Press, 1981.

———. *Presidential Campaigns.* New York: Oxford University Press, 1984.

Candidates '80. Washington: Congressional Quarterly Inc., 1980.

Candidates '84. Washington: Congressional Quarterly Inc., 1984.

Carter, Jimmy. *Keeping Faith: Memoirs of a President.* New York: Bantam, 1982.

Chamberlin, Hope. *A Minority of Members: Women in the U.S. Congress.* New York: Praeger Publishers, 1973.

Congressional Quarterly's Guide to Congress, 2nd ed. Washington: Congressional Quarterly Inc., 1976.

Drew, Elizabeth. *Portrait of an Election: The 1980 Presidential Campaign.* New York: Simon and Schuster, 1981.

Elections '80. Washington: Congressional Quarterly Inc., 1980.

Elections '82. Washington: Congressional Quarterly Inc., 1982.

Elections '84. Washington: Congressional Quarterly Inc., 1984.

Frank, Sid. *The Presidents: Tidbits and Trivia.* Maplewood, New Jersey: Hammond Incorporated, 1975.

Freidel, Frank. *The Presidents of the United States of America,* 9th ed. Washington: White House Historical Association, 1982.

Germond, Jack W., and Jules Witcover. *Blue Smoke and Mirrors: How Reagan Won and Carter Lost the Election of 1980.* New York: Viking Press, 1981.

Goldman, Ralph M. *The Democratic Party in American Politics.* New York: Macmillan, 1966.

Hoyt, Edwin P. *Jumbos and Jackasses: A Popular History of the Political Wars.* Garden City, New York: Doubleday, 1960.

Jensen, Amy. *The White House and Its Thirty-Five Families.* New York: McGraw-Hill, 1970.

Josephy, Alvin M., Jr. *On the Hill: A History of the American Congress.* New York: Simon and Schuster, 1979.

Kane, Joseph N. *Facts About the Presidents,* 4th ed. New York: H. W. Wilson Company, 1981.

Kennedy, John F. *Profiles in Courage.* New York: Harper and Row, 1961.

Lash, Joseph S. *Eleanor and Franklin.* New York: Norton, 1971.

Lindop, Edmund. *The First Book of Elections,* Rev. ed. New York: Franklin Watts, 1972.

——. "A National Need: Music and the Presidents." *American History Illustrated,* December, 1975.

——, and Joseph Jares. *White House Sportsmen.* Boston: Houghton Mifflin, 1964.

Manchester, William. *One Brief Shining Moment: Remembering Kennedy.* Boston: Little, Brown, 1983.

McConnell, Jane and Burt. *Our First Ladies*. New York: Crowell, 1953.

Means, Marianne. *The Women in the White House: The Lives, Times, and Influences of Twelve Notable First Ladies*. New York: Random House, 1963.

Moses, John B., and Wilbur Cross. *Presidential Courage*. New York: Norton, 1980.

National Party Conventions, 1831-1980. Washington: Congressional Quarterly Inc., 1983.

Parmet, Herbert S. *The Democrats: The Years After F.D.R.* New York: Macmillan, 1976.

Pious, Richard M. *The American Presidency*. New York: Basic Books, 1979.

President Carter 1980. Washington: Congressional Quarterly Inc., 1981.

Presidential Elections Since 1789. Washington: Congressional Quarterly Inc., 1983.

Reeves, Richard. *Convention*. New York: Harcourt Brace Jovanovich, 1977.

Remini, Robert Vincent. *Martin Van Buren and the Making of the Democratic Party*. New York: Norton, 1970.

Roseboom, Eugene H., and Alfred E. Eckles, Jr. *A History of Presidential Elections from George Washington to Jimmy Carter*, 4th ed. New York: Macmillan, 1979.

Russell, Francis. *Presidential Makers from Mark Hanna to Joseph P. Kennedy*. Boston: Little, Brown, 1976.

Scammon, Richard, compiler. *America at the Polls*. Pittsburgh: University of Pittsburgh Press, 1965.

Schlesinger, Arthur M., Jr., ed. *History of U.S. Political Parties*. New York: Chelsea House, 1973.

Shenkman, Richard, and Kurt Reiger. *One-Night Stands with American History*. New York: Morrow, 1980.

Simon, Paul. *The Once and Future Democrats: Strategies for Change*. New York: Continuum, 1982.

White, Theodore. *America in Search of Itself: The Making of the President, 1956-1980*. New York: Harper and Row, 1982.

Witcover, Jules. *Marathon: The Pursuit of the Presidency*. New York: Viking Press, 1977.

Wooten, James. *Dasher: The Roots and the Rising of Jimmy Carter*. New York: Summit Books, 1978.

INDEX